Practice for
HIGH SCHOOL COMPETENCY TESTS IN ENGLISH

Editorial Staff of Scholastic Testing Service, Inc.

ARCO PUBLISHING, INC.
NEW YORK

Published by Arco Publishing, Inc.
215 Park Avenue South, New York, N.Y. 10003

Library of Congress Cataloging in Publication Data
Main entry under title:

Practice for high school competency tests in
   English (reading and writing skills)

   Summary: Two sample tests for practice in language
arts, emphasizing comprehension of facts and ability to
draw conclusions from reading.
   1. English language—Composition and exercises—
Examinations, questions, etc.   2. Reading—Examinations,
questions, etc.   [1. English language—Composition
and exercises—Examinations, questions, etc.
2. Reading—Examinations, questions, etc.]   I. Scholastic
Testing Service.

PE1413.P68   1983   428.4'076   82-24313
ISBN 0-668-05550-2 (pbk.)

Printed in the United States of America

CONTENTS

7062186

Introduction

This book was designed to help students preparing to take a Language competency test. A competency test may be called an "Assessment Test," a "Minimum Basic Skills Test," a "Minimum Competency Test," or a "Survival Skills Test." What are these tests all about? The purpose of a competency test is to measure an individual's *minimum* level of achievement in areas regarded essential to living in our modern society. Of course, the meaning of "essential" may change according to who is using it, but certain language skills, such as comprehension of facts and ability to draw conclusions from reading, are generally accepted as essential. Many test items are based on encounters in the adult world, such as filling out a job application, reading a newspaper, etc., because the ability to deal with these encounters *is* essential in today's world.

Whether it is administered by the state or by local school districts, some kind of competency testing program is used by most American states. Students at any grade level may be tested to determine the level of competency they have reached or how well they have mastered the material considered appropriate for that grade level. Many high schools now require competency tests as a requirement for graduation, so students in grades 9 through 12 are tested most often.

Educators and many other people with an interest in education have often discussed the topic: Why is competency testing important? The purpose of competency testing is not to test students about everything they have learned during their school years. The purpose of competency testing is to test students for a minimum level of achievement, for what is considered the very least a high school senior should know upon graduating. The student who passes a competency test can feel reasonably prepared to face certain situations in the adult world. Many high school seniors have no difficulty at all with competency tests. Educators can use competency testing as a tool for evaluating the quality of education in their district, city, or state. The community can consider it an aid to assimilating teenagers into the adult world.

What is a passing score on a competency test? There are three ways this can be determined. The first is to establish a certain percentage of correct answers as a passing score. By calculating the percentage of questions you answered correctly, and comparing it to the pre-established passing score, you can see how well you did. For example, if 75% is considered a passing score, and you correctly answered 150 of 200 questions, you passed the test.

Competency tests are written to certain specifications, checking performance on various objectives. Another method for determining achievement is by measuring performance on each test objective. The Language competency tests in this book were written with various objectives in mind. Each objective is tested with at least two items per test. The content outline which follows each sample test provides a list of the objectives and specifies the items that test each objective. Correctly answering two questions for each objective may be the requirement for a passing score.

Another possible method of calculating achievement combines the first two methods. For example, the requirement for a passing score might be to correctly answer two of the questions for 80% of the objectives on the test.

Prior to taking a competency test, the student may or may not know what is expected for a passing grade. It is to the student's advantage to do the best he or she can. A competency test is not designed to determine which students are poorer or better than others, so students should not feel a need to compete against one another. Competency tests are designed so that all average students can potentially pass them.

There are two separate Language tests in this book. Each section has a set of directions. Between the two tests is a study guide for improving your test scores. Following the content outline by objective, the guide explains the objective and types of items that test the objective and provides sample items and suggestions for additional practice. By using the study guide, a student may learn how to handle something he or she was not familiar with. Additional practice will prove helpful in improving understanding as well as scores. Parents and teachers may provide additional assistance if necessary.

Students should relax when taking a competency test (or any other test). Read this book carefully — work all the problems on both tests, and use the study guide to help you improve in those areas that were difficult for you. Then you will be well-prepared to take a competency test. Go to the test well-rested and relaxed, and do the best you can.

Questions on a Language competency test are very much like questions on any other kind of language skills test. However, a competency test covers a much broader scope of material, so you will be tested on material you studied several years ago as well as on material you studied recently. Some of the questions on this competency test are about life skills, such as using reference sources, reading, and filling out forms. The content outline provides a full list of the topics covered on the tests in this book. The sample test items present a wide variety of questions. All competency tests will not be alike, but these are a good guide to what you may expect to find.

To prepare for these language competency tests, follow these simple steps:

1. Carefully cut or tear out the answer sheets on pages 7 and 9.
    One of these is for Form A of the test, and one is for Form B.
    The extra ones on pages 11 and 13 are for later use.

    Answer sheets such as these are usually scored by machines,
    so you *must* mark them carefully and accurately if you
    want to get full credit for your work.

    Using a soft-lead No. 2 pencil, fill out the information
    needed. Print your name in the boxes headed "NAME."
    Start in the first box and print your last name first,
    putting one letter in each box. At the end of your last
    name, skip a box and print your first name (or as much
    of it as will fit). Print your middle initial in the box
    labeled "MI." Now, fill in the circle under each box that
    has the same letter in it as the box. Fill in the blank circle
    under a blank box. Completely fill in the circles with
    heavy, dark marks. Thoroughly erase any mistakes you
    might have made.

Now fill in the circle marked "Girl" or "Boy" as appropriate. Print the name of your school, grade, section (if any), city, state, the subject tested, and the test form. Mark "TEST FORM" "A" for the first test and "B" for the second test.

2. Start with the Form A test. Read each question carefully and choose the best answer (each question has four answer choices — "a," "b," "c," "d"). Mark the letter of the best answer by filling in the circle with that letter next to the question number on the answer sheet. Be sure to work the entire test — there are 200 questions on each form.

3. When you have finished taking Form A of the test, check your answers against the Form A answer key on page 62. Circle or put a check next to any incorrect answers on your answer sheet and mark the correct answer. (For the Form B test, check your answers against the Form B answer key on page 152.)

4. Now check the content outline beginning on page 65 (155 for Form B). Put a circle around the numbers of the questions you incorrectly answered.

5. Now turn to the Study Guide for Better Scores starting on page 67. Using the content outline you just marked, find the section of the study guide that deals with the types of questions you missed. Read the study guide carefully and work the sample problems. If you are still having trouble understanding something, ask a parent or teacher to help you. Only read those sections of the study guide that apply to the objectives with which you are having trouble.

6.   Now follow steps 1-5, using the Form B test.

7.   If you have completed steps 1-6 above and need additional help, read through the entire study guide and work all the sample problems. Using the extra answer sheets that have been provided, take each test a second time. Then repeat the procedures outlined above. This will help you determine the areas in which you have shown improvement and the areas in which you need to develop your skills.

STS—ANALYSIS OF SKILLS

NAME

Boy ○ Girl ○

SCHOOL _____ GRADE _____ SECTION _____

CITY _____ STATE _____

SUBJECT TESTED _____ TEST LEVEL _____ TEST FORM _____

BEGIN TEST HERE

7

DO NOT
WRITE
IN THIS
SPACE

131 ⓐ ⓑ ⓒ ⓓ
132 ⓐ ⓑ ⓒ ⓓ
133 ⓐ ⓑ ⓒ ⓓ
134 ⓐ ⓑ ⓒ ⓓ
135 ⓐ ⓑ ⓒ ⓓ
136 ⓐ ⓑ ⓒ ⓓ
137 ⓐ ⓑ ⓒ ⓓ
138 ⓐ ⓑ ⓒ ⓓ
139 ⓐ ⓑ ⓒ ⓓ
140 ⓐ ⓑ ⓒ ⓓ
141 ⓐ ⓑ ⓒ ⓓ
142 ⓐ ⓑ ⓒ ⓓ
143 ⓐ ⓑ ⓒ ⓓ
144 ⓐ ⓑ ⓒ ⓓ
145 ⓐ ⓑ ⓒ ⓓ
146 ⓐ ⓑ ⓒ ⓓ
147 ⓐ ⓑ ⓒ ⓓ
148 ⓐ ⓑ ⓒ ⓓ
149 ⓐ ⓑ ⓒ ⓓ
150 ⓐ ⓑ ⓒ ⓓ

151 ⓐ ⓑ ⓒ ⓓ
152 ⓐ ⓑ ⓒ ⓓ
153 ⓐ ⓑ ⓒ ⓓ
154 ⓐ ⓑ ⓒ ⓓ
155 ⓐ ⓑ ⓒ ⓓ
156 ⓐ ⓑ ⓒ ⓓ
157 ⓐ ⓑ ⓒ ⓓ
158 ⓐ ⓑ ⓒ ⓓ
159 ⓐ ⓑ ⓒ ⓓ
160 ⓐ ⓑ ⓒ ⓓ
161 ⓐ ⓑ ⓒ ⓓ
162 ⓐ ⓑ ⓒ ⓓ
163 ⓐ ⓑ ⓒ ⓓ
164 ⓐ ⓑ ⓒ ⓓ
165 ⓐ ⓑ ⓒ ⓓ

166 ⓐ ⓑ ⓒ ⓓ
167 ⓐ ⓑ ⓒ ⓓ
168 ⓐ ⓑ ⓒ ⓓ
169 ⓐ ⓑ ⓒ ⓓ
170 ⓐ ⓑ ⓒ ⓓ
171 ⓐ ⓑ ⓒ ⓓ
172 ⓐ ⓑ ⓒ ⓓ
173 ⓐ ⓑ ⓒ ⓓ
174 ⓐ ⓑ ⓒ ⓓ
175 ⓐ ⓑ ⓒ ⓓ
176 ⓐ ⓑ ⓒ ⓓ
177 ⓐ ⓑ ⓒ ⓓ
178 ⓐ ⓑ ⓒ ⓓ
179 ⓐ ⓑ ⓒ ⓓ
180 ⓐ ⓑ ⓒ ⓓ
181 ⓐ ⓑ ⓒ ⓓ
182 ⓐ ⓑ ⓒ ⓓ
183 ⓐ ⓑ ⓒ ⓓ
184 ⓐ ⓑ ⓒ ⓓ
185 ⓐ ⓑ ⓒ ⓓ

186 ⓐ ⓑ ⓒ ⓓ
187 ⓐ ⓑ ⓒ ⓓ
188 ⓐ ⓑ ⓒ ⓓ
189 ⓐ ⓑ ⓒ ⓓ
190 ⓐ ⓑ ⓒ ⓓ
191 ⓐ ⓑ ⓒ ⓓ
192 ⓐ ⓑ ⓒ ⓓ
193 ⓐ ⓑ ⓒ ⓓ
194 ⓐ ⓑ ⓒ ⓓ
195 ⓐ ⓑ ⓒ ⓓ
196 ⓐ ⓑ ⓒ ⓓ
197 ⓐ ⓑ ⓒ ⓓ
198 ⓐ ⓑ ⓒ ⓓ
199 ⓐ ⓑ ⓒ ⓓ
200 ⓐ ⓑ ⓒ ⓓ

STOP

STS—ANALYSIS OF SKILLS

NAME

Boy ○ Girl ○

SCHOOL _____ GRADE _____ SECTION _____

CITY _____ STATE _____

SUBJECT TESTED _____ TEST LEVEL _____ TEST FORM _____

BEGIN TEST HERE

1 ⓐ ⓑ ⓒ ⓓ
2 ⓐ ⓑ ⓒ ⓓ
3 ⓐ ⓑ ⓒ ⓓ
4 ⓐ ⓑ ⓒ ⓓ
5 ⓐ ⓑ ⓒ ⓓ
6 ⓐ ⓑ ⓒ ⓓ
7 ⓐ ⓑ ⓒ ⓓ
8 ⓐ ⓑ ⓒ ⓓ
9 ⓐ ⓑ ⓒ ⓓ
10 ⓐ ⓑ ⓒ ⓓ
11 ⓐ ⓑ ⓒ ⓓ
12 ⓐ ⓑ ⓒ ⓓ
13 ⓐ ⓑ ⓒ ⓓ
14 ⓐ ⓑ ⓒ ⓓ
15 ⓐ ⓑ ⓒ ⓓ
16 ⓐ ⓑ ⓒ ⓓ
17 ⓐ ⓑ ⓒ ⓓ
18 ⓐ ⓑ ⓒ ⓓ
19 ⓐ ⓑ ⓒ ⓓ
20 ⓐ ⓑ ⓒ ⓓ
21 ⓐ ⓑ ⓒ ⓓ
22 ⓐ ⓑ ⓒ ⓓ
23 ⓐ ⓑ ⓒ ⓓ
24 ⓐ ⓑ ⓒ ⓓ
25 ⓐ ⓑ ⓒ ⓓ

26 ⓐ ⓑ ⓒ ⓓ
27 ⓐ ⓑ ⓒ ⓓ
28 ⓐ ⓑ ⓒ ⓓ
29 ⓐ ⓑ ⓒ ⓓ
30 ⓐ ⓑ ⓒ ⓓ
31 ⓐ ⓑ ⓒ ⓓ
32 ⓐ ⓑ ⓒ ⓓ
33 ⓐ ⓑ ⓒ ⓓ
34 ⓐ ⓑ ⓒ ⓓ
35 ⓐ ⓑ ⓒ ⓓ
36 ⓐ ⓑ ⓒ ⓓ
37 ⓐ ⓑ ⓒ ⓓ
38 ⓐ ⓑ ⓒ ⓓ
39 ⓐ ⓑ ⓒ ⓓ
40 ⓐ ⓑ ⓒ ⓓ
41 ⓐ ⓑ ⓒ ⓓ
42 ⓐ ⓑ ⓒ ⓓ
43 ⓐ ⓑ ⓒ ⓓ
44 ⓐ ⓑ ⓒ ⓓ
45 ⓐ ⓑ ⓒ ⓓ
46 ⓐ ⓑ ⓒ ⓓ
47 ⓐ ⓑ ⓒ ⓓ
48 ⓐ ⓑ ⓒ ⓓ
49 ⓐ ⓑ ⓒ ⓓ
50 ⓐ ⓑ ⓒ ⓓ
51 ⓐ ⓑ ⓒ ⓓ
52 ⓐ ⓑ ⓒ ⓓ
53 ⓐ ⓑ ⓒ ⓓ
54 ⓐ ⓑ ⓒ ⓓ
55 ⓐ ⓑ ⓒ ⓓ
56 ⓐ ⓑ ⓒ ⓓ
57 ⓐ ⓑ ⓒ ⓓ
58 ⓐ ⓑ ⓒ ⓓ
59 ⓐ ⓑ ⓒ ⓓ
60 ⓐ ⓑ ⓒ ⓓ

61 ⓐ ⓑ ⓒ ⓓ
62 ⓐ ⓑ ⓒ ⓓ
63 ⓐ ⓑ ⓒ ⓓ
64 ⓐ ⓑ ⓒ ⓓ
65 ⓐ ⓑ ⓒ ⓓ
66 ⓐ ⓑ ⓒ ⓓ
67 ⓐ ⓑ ⓒ ⓓ
68 ⓐ ⓑ ⓒ ⓓ
69 ⓐ ⓑ ⓒ ⓓ
70 ⓐ ⓑ ⓒ ⓓ
71 ⓐ ⓑ ⓒ ⓓ
72 ⓐ ⓑ ⓒ ⓓ
73 ⓐ ⓑ ⓒ ⓓ
74 ⓐ ⓑ ⓒ ⓓ
75 ⓐ ⓑ ⓒ ⓓ
76 ⓐ ⓑ ⓒ ⓓ
77 ⓐ ⓑ ⓒ ⓓ
78 ⓐ ⓑ ⓒ ⓓ
79 ⓐ ⓑ ⓒ ⓓ
80 ⓐ ⓑ ⓒ ⓓ
81 ⓐ ⓑ ⓒ ⓓ
82 ⓐ ⓑ ⓒ ⓓ
83 ⓐ ⓑ ⓒ ⓓ
84 ⓐ ⓑ ⓒ ⓓ
85 ⓐ ⓑ ⓒ ⓓ
86 ⓐ ⓑ ⓒ ⓓ
87 ⓐ ⓑ ⓒ ⓓ
88 ⓐ ⓑ ⓒ ⓓ
89 ⓐ ⓑ ⓒ ⓓ
90 ⓐ ⓑ ⓒ ⓓ
91 ⓐ ⓑ ⓒ ⓓ
92 ⓐ ⓑ ⓒ ⓓ
93 ⓐ ⓑ ⓒ ⓓ
94 ⓐ ⓑ ⓒ ⓓ
95 ⓐ ⓑ ⓒ ⓓ

96 ⓐ ⓑ ⓒ ⓓ
97 ⓐ ⓑ ⓒ ⓓ
98 ⓐ ⓑ ⓒ ⓓ
99 ⓐ ⓑ ⓒ ⓓ
100 ⓐ ⓑ ⓒ ⓓ
101 ⓐ ⓑ ⓒ ⓓ
102 ⓐ ⓑ ⓒ ⓓ
103 ⓐ ⓑ ⓒ ⓓ
104 ⓐ ⓑ ⓒ ⓓ
105 ⓐ ⓑ ⓒ ⓓ
106 ⓐ ⓑ ⓒ ⓓ
107 ⓐ ⓑ ⓒ ⓓ
108 ⓐ ⓑ ⓒ ⓓ
109 ⓐ ⓑ ⓒ ⓓ
110 ⓐ ⓑ ⓒ ⓓ
111 ⓐ ⓑ ⓒ ⓓ
112 ⓐ ⓑ ⓒ ⓓ
113 ⓐ ⓑ ⓒ ⓓ
114 ⓐ ⓑ ⓒ ⓓ
115 ⓐ ⓑ ⓒ ⓓ
116 ⓐ ⓑ ⓒ ⓓ
117 ⓐ ⓑ ⓒ ⓓ
118 ⓐ ⓑ ⓒ ⓓ
119 ⓐ ⓑ ⓒ ⓓ
120 ⓐ ⓑ ⓒ ⓓ
121 ⓐ ⓑ ⓒ ⓓ
122 ⓐ ⓑ ⓒ ⓓ
123 ⓐ ⓑ ⓒ ⓓ
124 ⓐ ⓑ ⓒ ⓓ
125 ⓐ ⓑ ⓒ ⓓ
126 ⓐ ⓑ ⓒ ⓓ
127 ⓐ ⓑ ⓒ ⓓ
128 ⓐ ⓑ ⓒ ⓓ
129 ⓐ ⓑ ⓒ ⓓ
130 ⓐ ⓑ ⓒ ⓓ

MI

AGE — Yr — Mo
ELEM. SCHOOL
OTHER CODES — 1 2 3 4 5 6 7 8
DO NOT WRITE IN THIS SPACE

Copyright © 1974, Scholastic Testing Service, Inc., Bensenville, Illinois

131 ⓐ ⓑ ⓒ ⓓ
132 ⓐ ⓑ ⓒ ⓓ
133 ⓐ ⓑ ⓒ ⓓ
134 ⓐ ⓑ ⓒ ⓓ
135 ⓐ ⓑ ⓒ ⓓ
136 ⓐ ⓑ ⓒ ⓓ
137 ⓐ ⓑ ⓒ ⓓ
138 ⓐ ⓑ ⓒ ⓓ
139 ⓐ ⓑ ⓒ ⓓ
140 ⓐ ⓑ ⓒ ⓓ
141 ⓐ ⓑ ⓒ ⓓ
142 ⓐ ⓑ ⓒ ⓓ
143 ⓐ ⓑ ⓒ ⓓ
144 ⓐ ⓑ ⓒ ⓓ
145 ⓐ ⓑ ⓒ ⓓ
146 ⓐ ⓑ ⓒ ⓓ
147 ⓐ ⓑ ⓒ ⓓ
148 ⓐ ⓑ ⓒ ⓓ
149 ⓐ ⓑ ⓒ ⓓ
150 ⓐ ⓑ ⓒ ⓓ

151 ⓐ ⓑ ⓒ ⓓ
152 ⓐ ⓑ ⓒ ⓓ
153 ⓐ ⓑ ⓒ ⓓ
154 ⓐ ⓑ ⓒ ⓓ
155 ⓐ ⓑ ⓒ ⓓ
156 ⓐ ⓑ ⓒ ⓓ
157 ⓐ ⓑ ⓒ ⓓ
158 ⓐ ⓑ ⓒ ⓓ
159 ⓐ ⓑ ⓒ ⓓ
160 ⓐ ⓑ ⓒ ⓓ
161 ⓐ ⓑ ⓒ ⓓ
162 ⓐ ⓑ ⓒ ⓓ
163 ⓐ ⓑ ⓒ ⓓ
164 ⓐ ⓑ ⓒ ⓓ
165 ⓐ ⓑ ⓒ ⓓ

166 ⓐ ⓑ ⓒ ⓓ
167 ⓐ ⓑ ⓒ ⓓ
168 ⓐ ⓑ ⓒ ⓓ
169 ⓐ ⓑ ⓒ ⓓ
170 ⓐ ⓑ ⓒ ⓓ
171 ⓐ ⓑ ⓒ ⓓ
172 ⓐ ⓑ ⓒ ⓓ
173 ⓐ ⓑ ⓒ ⓓ
174 ⓐ ⓑ ⓒ ⓓ
175 ⓐ ⓑ ⓒ ⓓ
176 ⓐ ⓑ ⓒ ⓓ
177 ⓐ ⓑ ⓒ ⓓ
178 ⓐ ⓑ ⓒ ⓓ
179 ⓐ ⓑ ⓒ ⓓ
180 ⓐ ⓑ ⓒ ⓓ
181 ⓐ ⓑ ⓒ ⓓ
182 ⓐ ⓑ ⓒ ⓓ
183 ⓐ ⓑ ⓒ ⓓ
184 ⓐ ⓑ ⓒ ⓓ
185 ⓐ ⓑ ⓒ ⓓ

186 ⓐ ⓑ ⓒ ⓓ
187 ⓐ ⓑ ⓒ ⓓ
188 ⓐ ⓑ ⓒ ⓓ
189 ⓐ ⓑ ⓒ ⓓ
190 ⓐ ⓑ ⓒ ⓓ
191 ⓐ ⓑ ⓒ ⓓ
192 ⓐ ⓑ ⓒ ⓓ
193 ⓐ ⓑ ⓒ ⓓ
194 ⓐ ⓑ ⓒ ⓓ
195 ⓐ ⓑ ⓒ ⓓ
196 ⓐ ⓑ ⓒ ⓓ
197 ⓐ ⓑ ⓒ ⓓ
198 ⓐ ⓑ ⓒ ⓓ
199 ⓐ ⓑ ⓒ ⓓ
200 ⓐ ⓑ ⓒ ⓓ

STOP

STS—ANALYSIS OF SKILLS

NAME

Boy ○ Girl ○

SCHOOL _____ GRADE _____ SECTION _____

CITY _____ STATE _____

SUBJECT TESTED _____ TEST LEVEL _____ TEST FORM _____

BEGIN TEST HERE

AGE — Yr. Mo. ELEM. SCHOOL OTHER CODES 1 2 3 4 5 6 7 8

DO NOT WRITE IN THIS SPACE

11

DO NOT
WRITE
IN THIS
SPACE

131 ⓐ ⓑ ⓒ ⓓ
132 ⓐ ⓑ ⓒ ⓓ
133 ⓐ ⓑ ⓒ ⓓ
134 ⓐ ⓑ ⓒ ⓓ
135 ⓐ ⓑ ⓒ ⓓ
136 ⓐ ⓑ ⓒ ⓓ
137 ⓐ ⓑ ⓒ ⓓ
138 ⓐ ⓑ ⓒ ⓓ
139 ⓐ ⓑ ⓒ ⓓ
140 ⓐ ⓑ ⓒ ⓓ
141 ⓐ ⓑ ⓒ ⓓ
142 ⓐ ⓑ ⓒ ⓓ
143 ⓐ ⓑ ⓒ ⓓ
144 ⓐ ⓑ ⓒ ⓓ
145 ⓐ ⓑ ⓒ ⓓ
146 ⓐ ⓑ ⓒ ⓓ
147 ⓐ ⓑ ⓒ ⓓ
148 ⓐ ⓑ ⓒ ⓓ
149 ⓐ ⓑ ⓒ ⓓ
150 ⓐ ⓑ ⓒ ⓓ

151 ⓐ ⓑ ⓒ ⓓ
152 ⓐ ⓑ ⓒ ⓓ
153 ⓐ ⓑ ⓒ ⓓ
154 ⓐ ⓑ ⓒ ⓓ
155 ⓐ ⓑ ⓒ ⓓ
156 ⓐ ⓑ ⓒ ⓓ
157 ⓐ ⓑ ⓒ ⓓ
158 ⓐ ⓑ ⓒ ⓓ
159 ⓐ ⓑ ⓒ ⓓ
160 ⓐ ⓑ ⓒ ⓓ
161 ⓐ ⓑ ⓒ ⓓ
162 ⓐ ⓑ ⓒ ⓓ
163 ⓐ ⓑ ⓒ ⓓ
164 ⓐ ⓑ ⓒ ⓓ
165 ⓐ ⓑ ⓒ ⓓ

166 ⓐ ⓑ ⓒ ⓓ
167 ⓐ ⓑ ⓒ ⓓ
168 ⓐ ⓑ ⓒ ⓓ
169 ⓐ ⓑ ⓒ ⓓ
170 ⓐ ⓑ ⓒ ⓓ
171 ⓐ ⓑ ⓒ ⓓ
172 ⓐ ⓑ ⓒ ⓓ
173 ⓐ ⓑ ⓒ ⓓ
174 ⓐ ⓑ ⓒ ⓓ
175 ⓐ ⓑ ⓒ ⓓ
176 ⓐ ⓑ ⓒ ⓓ
177 ⓐ ⓑ ⓒ ⓓ
178 ⓐ ⓑ ⓒ ⓓ
179 ⓐ ⓑ ⓒ ⓓ
180 ⓐ ⓑ ⓒ ⓓ
181 ⓐ ⓑ ⓒ ⓓ
182 ⓐ ⓑ ⓒ ⓓ
183 ⓐ ⓑ ⓒ ⓓ
184 ⓐ ⓑ ⓒ ⓓ
185 ⓐ ⓑ ⓒ ⓓ

186 ⓐ ⓑ ⓒ ⓓ
187 ⓐ ⓑ ⓒ ⓓ
188 ⓐ ⓑ ⓒ ⓓ
189 ⓐ ⓑ ⓒ ⓓ
190 ⓐ ⓑ ⓒ ⓓ
191 ⓐ ⓑ ⓒ ⓓ
192 ⓐ ⓑ ⓒ ⓓ
193 ⓐ ⓑ ⓒ ⓓ
194 ⓐ ⓑ ⓒ ⓓ
195 ⓐ ⓑ ⓒ ⓓ
196 ⓐ ⓑ ⓒ ⓓ
197 ⓐ ⓑ ⓒ ⓓ
198 ⓐ ⓑ ⓒ ⓓ
199 ⓐ ⓑ ⓒ ⓓ
200 ⓐ ⓑ ⓒ ⓓ

STOP

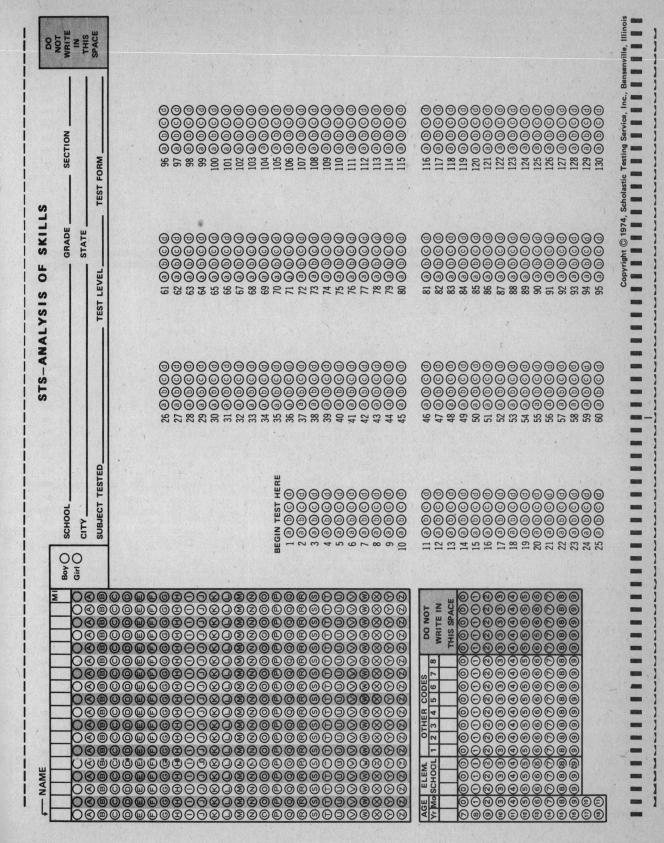

STS—ANALYSIS OF SKILLS

NAME

Boy ◯   Girl ◯

SCHOOL
CITY
SUBJECT TESTED

GRADE _____   SECTION _____
STATE
TEST LEVEL _____   TEST FORM _____

Copyright © 1974, Scholastic Testing Service, Inc., Bensenville, Illinois

13

131 ⓐ ⓑ ⓒ ⓓ
132 ⓐ ⓑ ⓒ ⓓ
133 ⓐ ⓑ ⓒ ⓓ
134 ⓐ ⓑ ⓒ ⓓ
135 ⓐ ⓑ ⓒ ⓓ
136 ⓐ ⓑ ⓒ ⓓ
137 ⓐ ⓑ ⓒ ⓓ
138 ⓐ ⓑ ⓒ ⓓ
139 ⓐ ⓑ ⓒ ⓓ
140 ⓐ ⓑ ⓒ ⓓ
141 ⓐ ⓑ ⓒ ⓓ
142 ⓐ ⓑ ⓒ ⓓ
143 ⓐ ⓑ ⓒ ⓓ
144 ⓐ ⓑ ⓒ ⓓ
145 ⓐ ⓑ ⓒ ⓓ
146 ⓐ ⓑ ⓒ ⓓ
147 ⓐ ⓑ ⓒ ⓓ
148 ⓐ ⓑ ⓒ ⓓ
149 ⓐ ⓑ ⓒ ⓓ
150 ⓐ ⓑ ⓒ ⓓ

151 ⓐ ⓑ ⓒ ⓓ
152 ⓐ ⓑ ⓒ ⓓ
153 ⓐ ⓑ ⓒ ⓓ
154 ⓐ ⓑ ⓒ ⓓ
155 ⓐ ⓑ ⓒ ⓓ
156 ⓐ ⓑ ⓒ ⓓ
157 ⓐ ⓑ ⓒ ⓓ
158 ⓐ ⓑ ⓒ ⓓ
159 ⓐ ⓑ ⓒ ⓓ
160 ⓐ ⓑ ⓒ ⓓ
161 ⓐ ⓑ ⓒ ⓓ
162 ⓐ ⓑ ⓒ ⓓ
163 ⓐ ⓑ ⓒ ⓓ
164 ⓐ ⓑ ⓒ ⓓ
165 ⓐ ⓑ ⓒ ⓓ

166 ⓐ ⓑ ⓒ ⓓ
167 ⓐ ⓑ ⓒ ⓓ
168 ⓐ ⓑ ⓒ ⓓ
169 ⓐ ⓑ ⓒ ⓓ
170 ⓐ ⓑ ⓒ ⓓ
171 ⓐ ⓑ ⓒ ⓓ
172 ⓐ ⓑ ⓒ ⓓ
173 ⓐ ⓑ ⓒ ⓓ
174 ⓐ ⓑ ⓒ ⓓ
175 ⓐ ⓑ ⓒ ⓓ
176 ⓐ ⓑ ⓒ ⓓ
177 ⓐ ⓑ ⓒ ⓓ
178 ⓐ ⓑ ⓒ ⓓ
179 ⓐ ⓑ ⓒ ⓓ
180 ⓐ ⓑ ⓒ ⓓ
181 ⓐ ⓑ ⓒ ⓓ
182 ⓐ ⓑ ⓒ ⓓ
183 ⓐ ⓑ ⓒ ⓓ
184 ⓐ ⓑ ⓒ ⓓ
185 ⓐ ⓑ ⓒ ⓓ

186 ⓐ ⓑ ⓒ ⓓ
187 ⓐ ⓑ ⓒ ⓓ
188 ⓐ ⓑ ⓒ ⓓ
189 ⓐ ⓑ ⓒ ⓓ
190 ⓐ ⓑ ⓒ ⓓ
191 ⓐ ⓑ ⓒ ⓓ
192 ⓐ ⓑ ⓒ ⓓ
193 ⓐ ⓑ ⓒ ⓓ
194 ⓐ ⓑ ⓒ ⓓ
195 ⓐ ⓑ ⓒ ⓓ
196 ⓐ ⓑ ⓒ ⓓ
197 ⓐ ⓑ ⓒ ⓓ
198 ⓐ ⓑ ⓒ ⓓ
199 ⓐ ⓑ ⓒ ⓓ
200 ⓐ ⓑ ⓒ ⓓ

STOP

Choose the word or phrase that means the same or about the same as the <u>underlined</u> word.

1. <u>spoiled</u> milk
   a) scalded
   b) fresh
   c) flavored
   d) rotten

2. try to <u>protect</u>
   a) caution
   b) guard
   c) watch
   d) attack

3. a dangerous <u>enemy</u>
   a) opponent
   b) friend
   c) relative
   d) energy

4. an <u>exciting</u> movie
   a) dull
   b) thrilling
   c) funny
   d) sad

5. a <u>slight</u> child
   a) slender
   b) fat
   c) smart
   d) strong

6. the airplane's <u>roar</u>
   a) flight
   b) weight
   c) loud noise
   d) position

Go on to the next page.

7. an <u>average</u> student

    a) ordinary
    b) beautiful
    c) poor
    d) good

8. good <u>advice</u>

    a) thinking
    b) accident
    c) suggestion
    d) meal

9. a wordy <u>lecture</u>

    a) speech
    b) letter
    c) play
    d) joke

10. <u>astonish</u> the audience

    a) disappoint
    b) confuse
    c) entertain
    d) surprise

11. an <u>independent</u> country

    a) tiny
    b) populated
    c) self-governing
    d) related

12. a <u>splendid</u> performance

    a) glorious
    b) wicked
    c) surprise
    d) terrible

Go on to the next page.

13. to <u>celebrate</u> a birthday
    a) honor
    b) make famous
    c) age
    d) forget

14. serious <u>injury</u>
    a) accident
    b) crime
    c) harm
    d) importance

15. <u>caution</u> the truckdriver
    a) stop
    b) aid
    c) warn
    d) pick up

16. <u>domestic</u> wine from California
    a) native
    b) bitter
    c) foreign
    d) sweet

17. a <u>wealthy</u> uncle
    a) kindly
    b) rich
    c) ugly
    d) funny

18. a <u>naughty</u> boy
    a) quick
    b) good
    c) disobedient
    d) stupid

Go on to the next page.

19. pleasant <u>entertainment</u>

    a) amusement
    b) work
    c) reading
    d) rest

20. answer <u>honestly</u>

    a) completely
    b) truthfully
    c) falsely
    d) hopefully

21. a <u>generous</u> father

    a) friendly
    b) strict
    c) stingy
    d) unselfish

22. <u>attempt</u> to win

    a) try
    b) hope
    c) forget
    d) love

23. <u>belief</u> in their ability

    a) ignorance
    b) talent
    c) faith
    d) disgust

24. <u>hesitate</u> to speak

    a) remember
    b) be unwilling
    c) sit
    d) hide

Go on to the next page.

25. living in <u>poverty</u>

    a) sin
    b) need
    c) loneliness
    d) plenty

26. a <u>comfortable</u> chair

    a) pretty
    b) miserable
    c) hard
    d) cozy

27. an <u>urgent</u> warning

    a) careful
    b) unimportant
    c) thoughtful
    d) pressing

28. a <u>delicate</u> rose

    a) artificial
    b) red
    c) coarse
    d) fragile

29. endless <u>patience</u>

    a) energy
    b) endurance
    c) curiosity
    d) sadness

30. her single <u>ambition</u>

    a) talent
    b) plan
    c) goal
    d) mistake

Go on to the next page.

For questions 31 to 50, mark your answer sheet for the letter of the sentence that contains a spelling error.

31. a) He ate boiled carrots, potatoes, and cabbage.
    b) My family attended the funeral of the drowned nieghbor.
    c) A cough can be a serious illness in the cold weather.
    d) Americans eat pumpkin pie to celebrate Thanksgiving.

32. a) The janitor left an umbrella and a handkerchief in the factory.
    b) We faithfully listened to the excellent lecture.
    c) The author guessed the historical importance of the Indian-head nickel.
    d) She received a dimond ring that once belonged to a princess.

33. a) A financial article was included on the economics examination.
    b) The ski tournament was the most important athletic event of the year.
    c) She did an assortment of dance exercises to keep in shape.
    d) The superintendent gave the opening speech at Monday's lunchon.

34. a) Their marrage was both long and happy.
    b) The stand carries foreign-language newspapers.
    c) The cheerful artist rarely painted unhappy pictures.
    d) A magazine editor needs to be careful and precise.

35. a) The red bicycle is the most expensive one in the store.
    b) The sleaves of the little girl's dress were covered with chocolate.
    c) Boris lives in the largest continent, Asia.
    d) Please introduce me to all the members of your family.

Go on to the next page.

36. a) The neglected freight train was left abandoned.
    b) Find the height and length of these triangles.
    c) The patient doctor gave medicine to each sick person.
    d) They had an arguement about the article in the bulletin.

37. a) The squirrel collected an asortment of nuts to store for the winter.
    b) The gentleman wearing the green shirt is a dentist.
    c) Jack won first prize in the tennis tournament.
    d) Please leave your name, address, and phone number at the desk.

38. a) They're graduating from high school tomorrow evening.
    b) It is urgent that you come at once to fix the electrical wiring.
    c) The orginal painting sold for two thousand dollars.
    d) The teacher was favorably impressed with the test results.

39. a) The blizard left half the town homeless.
    b) I do not know whether or not to cancel the appointment.
    c) It was the attorney's judgment that the man was guilty.
    d) The tragic events occurred last week.

40. a) The cat was accustomed to sleeping most of the day.
    b) The battery was guaranted to work for three months.
    c) The girl lost most of her possessions in the flood.
    d) The class conducted several scientific experiments.

Go on to the next page.

41. a) The spoiled child ate all the chocolate candies.
    b) The picnic was held in August.
    c) Are you aquainted with my sister?
    d) All our canned goods are stored in the cellar.

42. a) The captain had no choice but to tell the truth.
    b) My cousin has been lonely ever since he moved to a new neighborhood.
    c) Jane wrote a report on the three largest American citys.
    d) The answers to the arithmetic problems are in the book.

43. a) My sister and I have separate bedrooms.
    b) The music was written for paino and flute.
    c) The cherry blossoms are beautiful.
    d) Bring an umbrella to the outdoor concert.

44. a) The shortest distance between two points is a straight line.
    b) Frogs use their tongues to capture insects.
    c) Kara's birthday is the fifteenth of July.
    d) Our neice is visiting us for the summer.

45. a) The guide led them down a dangerous path.
    b) The taller twin is a registared nurse.
    c) The guests stayed in the apartment above the garage.
    d) Carl's father runs his own business.

Go on to the next page.

46. a) The blue chair is the most comfortible.
     b) The zookeeper had to work most holidays.
     c) The senator was elected for a second term.
     d) I need to purchase shampoo and a brush.

47. a) We only use those dishes for special ocassions.
     b) The woman became anxious when her son failed to return home.
     c) The diameter of a circle is longer than the radius.
     d) The mouse disappeared behind the cabinet.

48. a) My brother went on a hiking expedition with his college.
     b) The boat's anchor got caught in the grasses.
     c) The robber was desparate and frightened.
     d) The deer disappeared into the dark forest.

49. a) Louis represents our class on the student council.
     b) I complained to the managment because the store would not accept my check.
     c) Our national anthem is a pretty song.
     d) Peg's favorite movie is playing at a nearby theater.

50. a) There were seven loads of laundry to be washed.
     b) Three cows supply the entire family with all their milk.
     c) Ralph made a large deposit at the bank.
     d) The visiters come from all fifty states.

Go on to the next page.

For questions 51 to 90, look for errors in capitalization, punctuation, or usage. If there is no mistake, mark "d" on your answer sheet.

51. a) Mr. Cortes mowed his lawn in one hour.
    b) The wind blew Bens mittens down the street.
    c) The bus stopped for him and me.
    d) No mistakes.

52. a) Why don't you visit the old mill?
    b) Martin, Sam, and I are the fastest swimmers in our school.
    c) Celia collects rocks shells, and butterflies.
    d) No mistakes.

53. a) The book was too difficult for we students.
    b) Don't eat the cake we made for the party.
    c) The package, a heavy one, was delivered by messenger.
    d) No mistakes.

54. a) That group of birds makes a lot of noise in the morning.
    b) Renee was born on May 18, 1964.
    c) Winston doesn't play the french horn very well.
    d) No mistakes.

Go on to the next page.

55. a) We have taken the wrong route to California.
    b) He divided the presents equally among the four children.
    c) Yesterday Carla said, I may be late for school on Thursday."
    d) No mistakes.

56. a) Mrs. Conti, my teacher, is an excellent speaker.
    b) One of my favorite countries are Mexico.
    c) Claire took us to the amusement park.
    d) No mistakes.

57. a) I don't need any more cake or ice cream.
    b) I don't want to go to the museum no more.
    c) Neither Walter nor his sister is in the chorus.
    d) No mistakes.

58. a) The judges couldn't decide between the rocket model or the experiment.
    b) The concert, however, won't be canceled because of bad weather.
    c) The birds must fly south, or else they will die.
    d) No mistakes.

Go on to the next page.

59. a) The purple collage was the better in the exhibit.
     b) My horse, the brown jumper, is boarded in a nearby stable.
     c) Alex talked to him on the phone for over an hour.
     d) No mistakes.

60. a) Were going skiing and sledding when the weather turns cold.
     b) We will make an inspection even before the building is completed.
     c) Paul exclaimed, "Watch out for the truck!"
     d) No mistakes.

61. a) Kim and me are the best of friends.
     b) Her ring contained emeralds, rubies, and sapphires.
     c) I feel, Becky, that you need to work harder on your math.
     d) No mistakes.

62. a) Pass the salad to him.
     b) Sally asked, "when are we visiting the cranberry factory?"
     c) We painted with water colors, sculpted with clay, and sketched with charcoal in art class.
     d) No mistakes.

Go on to the next page.

63. a) Catherine gets up every morning at 7:10 a.m.
     b) After we finish lunch, we went to the swimming pool.
     c) Rachel invited Bob and me to dinner.
     d) No mistakes.

64. a) They're mailing the newspapers a week early.
     b) The doctor said to his patient, "It is important to get plenty of sleep."
     c) He addressed the book about languages to j. r. evans.
     d) No mistakes.

65. a) The paper doesn't have to be finished by Friday.
     b) The yellow one is the ripest of the dozen apples.
     c) Pat have driven to the airport to pick up her grandmother.
     d) No mistakes.

66. a) The soup tasted spicy.
     b) Silver necklaces were given to she and I.
     c) The children felt good after their entry won the contest.
     d) No mistakes.

Go on to the next page.

67. a) The poem "Summer in New York" won first prize in the poetry contest.
     b) Washington Irving wrote many fine books and tales such as "the legend of sleepy hollow."
     c) Rick asked the librarian, "Could you help me find some magazine articles about fishing?"
     d) No mistakes.

68. a) There are seven listings in the local telephone book for Beth A. Ryan.
     b) The new foreign students will arrive on monday by ship.
     c) Lisa called her new toy store that is located in the mall, Kids, Tots, and Co.
     d) No mistakes.

69. a) Carol and Sara swum thirty laps in the pool.
     b) The man himself rescued the baby from the burning house.
     c) Some plants in the garden don't get any water.
     d) No mistakes.

70. a) After the accident last winter, that car has never been the same.
     b) Mr. Thomas was relieved after he gave them the keys to the apartment.
     c) Tulips are beautiful flowers because of they're color.
     d) No mistakes.

Go on to the next page.

71. a) The race began at Lawrence ave., continued down the road along the river,
    and finished at the elementary school.
   b) The high school, bank, and steel plant will be closed on Memorial Day.
   c) Green grapes, purple grapes, and red grapes were included in the salad.
   d) No mistakes.

72. a) He is not here; perhaps you can reach him tomorrow.
   b) Today is their second wedding anniversary.
   c) The two of them went fishing at the pond.
   d) No mistakes.

73. a) The recipe calls for the following ingredients: milk, eggs, sugar, flour, butter.
   b) The book <u>The Life and Times of Mark Twain</u> is my favorite biography.
   c) Why don't you leave your cat with us Frances asked.
   d) No mistakes.

74. a) Do you know who George Sand is?
   b) That meal tasted good.
   c) All of us want to thank you for helping.
   d) No mistakes.

Go on to the next page.

75. a) Let's call cousin Ron in Nevada!
    b) Us and them have tickets for tonight's game.
    c) We met our friends at the skating rink.
    d) No mistakes.

76. a) What kind of car does she have?
    b) While washing some glasses, Matt dropped one and cut his hand.
    c) "What a beautiful star," Marie exclaimed.
    d) No mistakes.

77. a) My friend's two older brothers are Doctors.
    b) Both cheetahs and gazelles can run swiftly.
    c) Martha couldn't have jumped that far!
    d) No mistakes.

78. a) After we finished the chapter on algebra, the teacher taught us the principles of algebra.
    b) Anne danced well in that holiday ballet.
    c) Ever since we were in third grade, he and I, have been best friends.
    d) No mistakes.

Go on to the next page.

79. a) Henrik Ibsen wrote the play "the wild duck."
     b) Dr. Smith works at Ravenswood Hospital.
     c) Our parents are going skiing with us.
     d) No mistakes.

80. a) Set the package down in the dining room.
     b) Put those books in alphabetical order.
     c) Turn off the television before you leave the room.
     d) No mistakes.

81. a) You cannot go out until you finish your homework.
     b) We spent twelve hours at the amusement park.
     c) I are visiting relatives in Greece next summer.
     d) No mistakes.

82. a) She said, "we will be camping in Canada soon."
     b) The dance party begins at eight o'clock.
     c) Whether or not you join us, we are going to the show.
     d) No mistakes.

Go on to the next page.

83. a) Kay's birth certificate says she was born at 4:00 on Wednesday,
    September 8, 1979.
    b) After Lynn poured lighter fluid on the charcoal, she moved back to
    protect herself from the flames.
    c) Peter made his bed dusted his dresser and picked up his clothes before
    he left for the movies.
    d) No mistakes.

84. a) "Ain't this exciting?" asked Bobby.
    b) The movie is two-and-a-half hours long.
    c) They are walking to the library.
    d) No mistakes.

85. a) That foreign student speaks English good.
    b) The dog ran between the bushes.
    c) Traveling overseas must be very interesting.
    d) No mistakes.

86. a) The north and the south fought in the Civil War.
    b) That university is open six days a week.
    c) The state agency controls road repairs.
    d) No mistakes.

Go on to the next page.

87. a) Swimming and bicycling are good exercise.
     b) Each of the musicians were pleased with the performance.
     c) The captains decided among themselves which team would start.
     d) No mistakes.

88. a) The lost child was found in the toy department.
     b) Aren't those children home from school yet?
     c) I have lend that to you before.
     d) No mistakes.

89. a) Aren't these flowers beautiful?
     b) We haven't never been there before.
     c) He quickly made breakfast.
     d) No mistakes.

90. a) "Dinner will be served at seven," he said.
     b) Doesn't those pictures need to be framed for the holidays?
     c) Their house is three blocks north of mine.
     d) No mistakes.

Go on to the next page.

Read this passage, and then answer questions 91 to 98.

Walt Disney was a famous cartoonist who was best known for his two cartoon characters, Mickey Mouse and Donald Duck. He also produced television shows and motion pictures, and designed an amusement park. Disney was born in 1901 in Chicago. He studied at the Chicago Academy of Fine Arts. During World War I, he was an ambulance driver. After the war, he produced his first cartoon motion picture in Kansas City. In 1923, he moved to Hollywood where he invented the character Oswald the Rabbit. During World War II, Disney made training and information cartoons for the U.S. government.

Disney's first big success occurred in 1928 when he produced a Mickey Mouse film. In this film, Mickey talked. Soon he began producing cartoons in technicolor and, shortly afterwards, full-length movies such as "Fantasia," "Bambi," and "Cinderella." However, Disney was not content to produce only cartoons. He is also famous for his nature films and other movies. In 1950, he entered television and produced shows such as Mickey Mouse Club. In 1955, Disneyland, a large amusement park, opened. The cartoons of Disney are so famous and delightful that the United States government used Donald Duck to help sell Defense Bonds during World War II.

Go on to the next page.

91. What is the best title for this passage?

    a) "Disney's Contribution to World War II"
    b) "Cartoons and Movies"
    c) "Television in the 1950's"
    d) "The Work of Walt Disney"

92. Which cartoon character was Disney's first big success?

    a) Donald Duck
    b) Oswald the Rabbit
    c) Mickey Mouse
    d) Bambi

93. Where was Disney born?

    a) Hollywood
    b) Chicago
    c) Kansas City
    d) Germany

94. Which statement is true about Disney's television work?

    a) It is not important.
    b) He worked in television after he had experience working with movies.
    c) It was unsuccessful.
    d) He produced his television shows in Kansas City.

95. When did Disneyland open?

    a) 1901
    b) 1955
    c) 1950
    d) 1928

96. What did Disney do during World War II?

    a) write cartoons for a newspaper
    b) invent Donald Duck
    c) drive an ambulance
    d) produce information cartoons

97. What can you conclude about Walt Disney?

    a) He produced only Mickey Mouse and other cartoons.
    b) He had a long and varied career.
    c) He is responsible for all technicolor cartoons.
    d) He was not a good artist.

98. Why did the U.S. government use a Disney cartoon character to sell Defense Bonds?

    a) because Disney was active during World War I
    b) because everyone watched the Mickey Mouse Club
    c) because Disney produced many nature films
    d) because some Disney characters were familiar to everyone

Go on to the next page.

Read this passage, and then answer questions 99 to 106.

The pioneers of early America had to endure many hardships while they settled the land. Nature, while often their best friend, was also an enemy. Pioneers suffered through floods, droughts, sleet, heavy snows, sandstorms, tornadoes, intense heat, and extreme cold. Animals also brought trouble to these newly arrived people. Grasshoppers and locusts frequently destroyed the year's crops. Spiders, ticks, and flies caused pain to sleeping children. Herds of buffalo often stampeded and trampled to death anything in their path.

At first, infectious diseases were not a problem because the pioneers led such an isolated life. Women tended the sick without the aid of a doctor. They used home remedies such as cobwebs for bandages. Later, however, when more settlers arrived, many suffered from yellow fever and cholera.

Despite many hardships, the pioneers managed to have some fun. Men enjoyed target practice and tomahawk throwing. Work gave the people many opportunities for parties. Nutting parties, husking bees, log rollings, quilting parties, and wool-picking parties were popular. Neighbors helped newcomers build their barns and houses. Afterwards a big feast was given. People danced, played jokes, and told stories. Weddings were also fun for the pioneers. Sometimes jealous settlers not invited to the wedding would cut off the tails of the guests' horses.

Go on to the next page.

99. What is the best title for this passage?

    a) "Illness and the Pioneer"
    b) "Hardship and Fun for the Pioneer"
    c) "A Pioneer Wedding"
    d) "The Joys of Pioneer Life"

100. Which word best describes the pioneers' attitude toward a neighbor?

    a) generous
    b) jealous
    c) stingy
    d) hateful

101. Who was responsible for helping the sick in the pioneer family?

    a) fathers
    b) doctors
    c) women
    d) guests

102. Which of the following is not a hardship the pioneers had to face?

    a) storms
    b) insects
    c) barn building
    d) sickness

103. Which statement is true about pioneer fun and play?

    a) They enjoyed themselves only at weddings.
    b) They played all day long.
    c) They enjoyed combining work and play.
    d) They never danced.

104. When did pioneers often have a feast?

    a) when a doctor finally arrived
    b) after a tornado
    c) before they planted the year's crops
    d) after helping a neighbor build a barn

105. What might a pioneer do who was not invited to a wedding?

    a) chop off a horse's tail
    b) send the bride a grasshopper
    c) play a joke
    d) tell a story

106. How did the pioneers face the hardships of their life?

    a) by calling a doctor
    b) by giving up
    c) with bravery
    d) by moving back East

Go on to the next page.

Read this passage, and then answer questions 107 to 114.

Scientists have always known that people dance. People in every country of the world and throughout the ages have danced with others as a way of being friendly. There have been religious dances, war dances, political dances, and rain dances. But scientists are now discovering that even tiny infants and some apes know how to dance. A scientist named William Condon has discovered that human infants as young as twenty minutes go through a ritual dance following the speech of an adult. Condon discovered this infant dance by studying slow-motion movies of adults talking to infants. He observed the babies moving their limbs in exact synchrony with the words of the speaker. To him, the baby's movements looked just like a beautiful dance. If infants are in some way not allowed to experience this "dance," they can suffer from learning disabilities. Some new research even suggests that infants begin to dance while still in the womb.

However, human beings are not the only animals that dance. Chimpanzees of the Gombe Forest are known to partake in "rain dances." The chimps beat rhythmically on their chests and nearby objects. They stamp their feet, clap their hands, and twirl about in circles. Some gorillas have also been seen dancing. These animals move about as if drunk. From all these observations, scientists have concluded that dancing may have something to do with the evolution of man.

Go on to the next page.

107. What is the best title for this passage?

    a) "The Dancing Apes of the Gombe
       Forest"
    b) "Rain Dances"
    c) "Scientific Discoveries about Dance"
    d) "How Infants Dance"

108. How did William Condon discover that
     infants dance?

    a) by studying monkeys
    b) after visiting a day-care center
    c) by talking to doctors
    d) by studying slow-motion movies

109. What do infants do when they "dance"?

    a) stamp their feet
    b) clap their hands
    c) twirl in circles
    d) move in rhythm to speech

110. Dancing may help a human infant

    a) strengthen the leg muscles.
    b) appreciate music.
    c) do leg exercises.
    d) learn to talk.

111. Where do people dance?

    a) throughout the world
    b) only in Africa
    c) in most parts of the world
    d) only in slow-motion movies

112. Which statement is true about dancing?

    a) Many animals dance.
    b) Dance is important in helping
       infants learn.
    c) People danced only in the
       19th century.
    d) A few babies can learn to dance.

113. Which animal dances "rain dances"?

    a) chimps
    b) gorillas
    c) fish
    d) geese

114. Why have scientists concluded that dancing
     might have something to do with the
     evolution of man?

    a) because people dance to be friendly
    b) because only advanced animals can
       dance
    c) because infants can have learning
       disabilities
    d) because adults speak to babies

Go on to the next page.

Read this passage, and then answer questions 115 to 122.

Holly sat quietly on the bus as town after town passed by. She was hot and tired and longed for the tedious ride to come to an end. She felt like a caged bird. Every summer, Holly traveled from North Carolina to Prince Edward Island to visit her grandmother and younger cousin, Harrison. Prince Edward Island is a small Canadian province north of Maine that has the best potatoes and oysters in the whole world! Holly felt very hungry as she ate the cheese sandwich she had packed for the journey.

Holly fell asleep and when she awoke it was time to board the ferry boat that would take her to her destination. While she was on the boat, Holly imagined the activities of the coming day. She already felt cooler and more rested. The first thing she would do would be to take a swim. Although the air was cool on the island, the water was as warm as the water alongside Florida. Then she and Harrison would collect shells, hermit crabs, and sand shrimp. She had brought mostly old clothes because the red sandstone roads and beaches badly stained clothing. Harrison would then take her to the best mud flats where the two of them would stand up to their knees in cool mud and dig for clams. Because the clams could not move quickly in the dense mud, the cousins could fill up a bucket with clams in ten minutes. With mud drying on their feet, Holly and Harrison would walk barefoot to the pier to meet the lobster boats. There they would bargain with the fishermen to buy a few small lobsters. Home again, their grandmother would cook up a great chowder with the lobsters and clams plus potatoes and oysters.

Go on to the next page.

115. The best title for this passage would be

    a) "A Summer Trip."
    b) "Grandmother's Farm."
    c) "A Bus Ride."
    d) "Digging for Clams."

116. According to the story, what was life like on Prince Edward Island?

    a) informal
    b) quarrelsome
    c) expensive
    d) boring

117. Where is Prince Edward Island located?

    a) Canada
    b) Florida
    c) Maine
    d) North Carolina

118. What was meant by . . . she felt like a caged bird?

    a) She was afraid of birds.
    b) She was going to a bird sanctuary.
    c) She was restless.
    d) She was afraid to sing.

119. Which statement is true about Harrison?

    a) He lived in North Carolina.
    b) He was Holly's uncle.
    c) He was younger than Holly.
    d) He rode on the bus with Holly.

120. Who gathered many of the ingredients for the chowder?

    a) a fisherman
    b) Grandmother
    c) Holly and Harrison
    d) the bus driver

121. Where did the children find the clams?

    a) in the mud
    b) in the ocean
    c) at the pier
    d) in sandstone

122. How did Holly's mood change in the two paragraphs?

    a) She became relaxed.
    b) She became more hungry.
    c) She became seasick.
    d) She became sadder.

Go on to the next page.

Choose the list that shows the words in alphabetical order.

123. a) salary   b) sale   c) same   d) sale
a)	b)	c)	d)
salary	sale	same	sale
sale	same	sale	salary
salmon	salary	salary	salmon
salt	salmon	salt	salt
same	salt	salmon	same

124. a) ear   b) eagle   c) eager   d) ease
a)	b)	c)	d)
ear	eagle	eager	ease
eagle	eager	eagle	earth
earth	ear	ear	ear
eager	earth	earth	eagle
ease	ease	ease	eager

Go on to the next page.

Choose the listing from the telephone book that shows the names in alphabetical order.

125. a) Black, Clark J.
         Blankstein, Julius P.
         Blankstein, Robert
         Bloom, Irving R.
         Blume, Mary K.

      b) Black, Clark J.
         Blankstein, Robert
         Blankstein, Julius P.
         Bloom, Irving R.
         Blume, Mary K.

      c) Blankstein, Julius P.
         Black, Clark J.
         Blankstein, Robert
         Bloom, Irving R.
         Blume, Mary K.

      d) Black, Clark J.
         Blankstein, Julius P.
         Blankstein, Robert
         Blume, Mary K.
         Bloom, Irving R.

126. a) K-9 Inn
         Kats Lodge
         Ken's Dog Palace
         Kim's Animal Care
         Kittens & Puppies

      b) Kats Lodge
         K-9 Inn
         Ken's Dog Palace
         Kittens & Puppies
         Kim's Animal Care

      c) K-9 Inn
         Kats Lodge
         Ken's Dog Palace
         Kittens & Puppies
         Kim's Animal Care

      d) Kats Lodge
         K-9 Inn
         Ken's Dog Palace
         Kim's Animal Care
         Kittens & Puppies

Go on to the next page.

Use the instructions below to answer questions 127 to 130.

HOW TO MAKE A STRINGED INSTRUMENT

1. Gather together a wooden box, twelve nails, six rubber bands of various widths, a hammer, sandpaper, and a brush and paints.

2. Smooth any rough edges on the box with sandpaper.

3. Take a hammer and nail. Make six small holes equally spaced along one side of the box. Make six parallel holes along the other side of the box.

4. Take each nail and hammer it into a hole. There should be six nails on one side and six nails on the other side of the box.

5. Cut a rubber band and stretch it across the box. Secure each end of the rubber band to a nail. Do this with each rubber band. Remember a thicker rubber band will make a lower sound than a thin one. Arrange your rubber bands accordingly.

6. OPTIONAL: Paint the outside of the box.

---

127. It is <u>not</u> necessary to follow which step?

    a) step 4
    b) step 1
    c) step 3
    d) step 6

128. Larry's instrument has three thick rubber bands and three thin rubber bands. Which statement is true about Larry's instrument?

    a) His instrument can play only six identical notes.
    b) His instrument can produce three high sounds and three low sounds.
    c) His instrument can play only high notes.
    d) His instrument can produce no sound.

129. If you correctly follow the instructions, how many strings will your instrument have?

    a) 4
    b) 12
    c) 3
    d) 6

130. What is the first thing you must do to make your instrument?

    a) Use a hammer to make small holes.
    b) Sand the rough edges of the box.
    c) Hammer in the nails.
    d) Gather all the equipment.

Go on to the next page.

Use the table of contents below to answer questions 131 to 134.

TABLE OF CONTENTS

131. Chapter 3 of the novella begins on which page?

    a) page 4
    b) page 24
    c) page 14
    d) page 34

132. What is found on page 48?

    a) a story
    b) a mystery
    c) a novella
    d) a poem

133. Chapter 1 of the mystery begins on which page?

    a) page 34
    b) page 40
    c) page 35
    d) page 37

134. How many pages is "Vacation in Maine"?

    a) 5 pages
    b) 7 pages
    c) 10 pages
    d) 1 page

Go on to the next page.

135. Which reference source would you use to find the call number for the book *The Magic Years*?

    a) encyclopedia
    b) card catalog
    c) almanac
    d) dictionary

136. Which reference source would you use to find the number of syllables in the word "abdicate"?

    a) dictionary
    b) index
    c) thesaurus
    d) table of contents

137. Which reference source would best show you that the earth is a sphere?

    a) atlas
    b) globe
    c) dictionary
    d) world map

138. Which reference source would you use to find five synonyms for "red"?

    a) thesaurus
    b) dictionary
    c) glossary
    d) encyclopedia

139. Which reference source would tell you about four recent magazine articles about seals?

    a) encyclopedia
    b) *Guinness Book of World Records*
    c) *Readers' Guide to Periodical Literature*
    d) atlas

140. Which reference source would tell you what life was like in ancient Greece?

    a) encyclopedia
    b) dictionary
    c) atlas
    d) glossary

141. Which reference source would give the meaning of a difficult word used in a science textbook?

    a) title page
    b) table of contents
    c) glossary
    d) copyright date

142. Which reference source would have a list of several books about Iceland?

    a) card catalog
    b) encyclopedia
    c) dictionary
    d) *Readers' Guide to Periodical Literature*

Go on to the next page.

Use the dictionary page entries below to answer questions 143 to 146.

DICTIONARY PAGE

ov·en (uv´ən), *n.*, a vessel for heating, baking, or cooking.
o·ver·cast (ō´vər kast´), *n.* **1.** a covering of clouds. *adj.* **1.** coated. **2.** cloudy; dark.
o·ver·come (ō´vər kum´), *v.* **1.** to conquer. **2.** to master.
o·ver·crowd (ō´vər kroud´), *v.* to crowd too many people.

143. What part of speech is the word "overcast"?

　a) noun only
　b) noun and adjective
　c) verb
　d) adjective only

144. What is the second meaning for the word "overcome"?

　a) dark
　b) conquer
　c) master
　d) cloudy

145. How many syllables are in the word "overcrowd"?

　a) 1
　b) 2
　c) 3
　d) 4

146. On which syllable is the accent in the word "oven"?

　a) third
　b) second
　c) first
　d) fourth

Go on to the next page.

47

Use the index below to answer questions 147 to 150.

```
┌─────────────────────────────────────────────────┐
│                   BOOK INDEX                      │
│                                                   │
│   Capes. . . . . . . . . . . . . . . . . .  39-51 │
│       Cape Charles . . . . . . . . . .  39, 40, 50│
│       Cape Cod. . . . . . . . . . . . .  45-51    │
│       Cape Hatteras . . . . . . . . .  38, 39, 51 │
│   Islands. . . . . . . . . . . . . . . .  101-121 │
│       Australia . . . . . . . . . . . . .  101-112│
│       England. . . . . . . . . . . . .  101, 110, 120-121│
│       New Zealand . . . . . . . . . .  111, 112, 113│
│       Puerto Rico . . . . . . . . . . .  101-105  │
│   Peninsulas . . . . . . . . . . . . . .  74-89   │
│       Florida . . . . . . . . . . . . . .  74, 80, 85│
│       Italy . . . . . . . . . . . . . . .  81, 88-89│
└─────────────────────────────────────────────────┘
```

147. Which pages would tell you about Florida?

    a) 101-121
    b) 81, 88-89
    c) 74-89
    d) 74, 80, 85

148. To find out about several different capes, you would look on pages

    a) 101-121.
    b) 39-51.
    c) 39.
    d) 45-51.

149. To find the definition of a peninsula, you would look on pages

    a) 39-51.
    b) 74-89.
    c) 101-121.
    d) 111, 112, 113.

150. Which pages would tell you about Puerto Rico?

    a) 101-105
    b) 111, 112, 113
    c) 101, 110, 120-121
    d) 112

Go on to the next page.

Use the map below to answer questions 151 to 154.

VILLAGE OF EAST CANAL

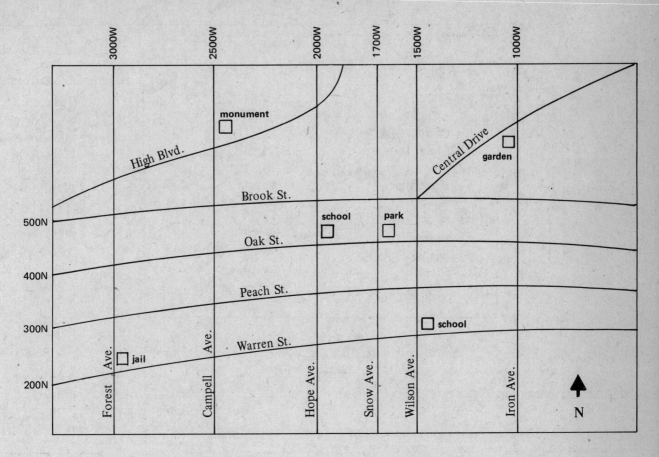

151. What is the number of Oak St. and Campell Ave.?

    a) 2500N and 400W
    b) 400N and 2500W
    c) 500N and 2500W
    d) 400N and 2000W

152. What is located at the corner of Forest Ave. and Warren St.?

    a) jail
    b) school
    c) garden
    d) monument

153. Which street is directly west of Snow Ave.?

    a) Hope Ave.
    b) Wilson Ave.
    c) Campell Ave.
    d) Iron Ave.

154. Which three streets does High Blvd. cross?

    a) Central Drive, Warren St., and Snow Ave.
    b) Brook, Oak, and Peach St.
    c) Forest, Snow, and Wilson Ave.
    d) Forest, Campell, and Hope Ave.

Go on to the next page.

Use the map below to answer questions 155 to 158.

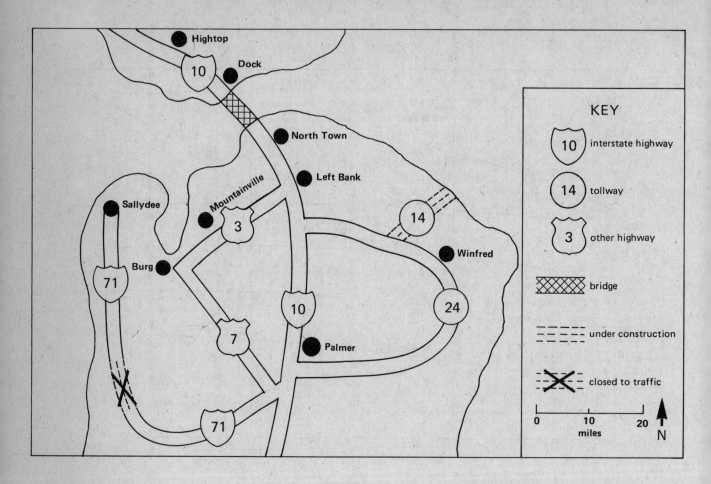

155. How many miles apart are Palmer and Left Bank?

    a) 25 miles
    b) 20 miles
    c) 40 miles
    d) 30 miles

156. Which highway has a section closed to traffic?

    a) Tollway 24
    b) Interstate 71
    c) Interstate 10
    d) Highway 3

157. What must you travel to go from Dock to North Town?

    a) a road closed to traffic
    b) a highway under construction
    c) a tollway
    d) a bridge

158. Which direction would you go to travel from Burg to Mountainville?

    a) southeast
    b) southwest
    c) northwest
    d) northeast

Go on to the next page.

Use the label below to answer questions 159 to 162.

CHILDREN'S ASPIRIN
liquid form

Dosage:

children under 2 years, only as directed by a physician

children 2 to 6 years, 1.4 ml (three droppers, fill to the top line)

Dosage may be given 2 or 3 times daily.

Drop dosage directly onto child's tongue, or mix with juice or other liquid.

Warning:
Do not administer for more than 7 days.

½ fl. oz. (15 ml)

159. What is the correct dosage for a one-year-old child?

   a) 1.4 ml
   b) ½ fl. oz.
   c) 15 ml
   d) only as directed by a physician

160. How often can this medicine be taken?

   a) only under the advice of a physician
   b) for 8 days
   c) 2 or 3 times daily
   d) every 2 or 3 hours

161. How much medicine should a five-year-old child take?

   a) three droppers filled to the top line
   b) 15 ml
   c) 14 ml
   d) ½ fl. oz.

162. How do the directions recommend giving the medicine?

   a) with a spoon
   b) mixed with juice
   c) by tablet
   d) only with a doctor's permission

Go on to the next page.

Use the label below to answer questions 163 to 166.

```
MACHINE   WASH   WARM
SEPARATELY. NO BLEACH.
TUMBLE  DRY  WARM.  DO
NOT DRY CLEAN OR IRON.
```

163. How should a garment with this label be washed?

   a) separately, in warm water
   b) in warm water with bleach
   c) in hot water
   d) by hand, in warm water

164. Paul is drying this garment with the dryer set on hot. What is he doing wrong?

   a) He should add bleach.
   b) He should not dry this piece of clothing.
   c) He should use a cold setting.
   d) He should set the dryer for warm.

165. What does the label not recommend?

   a) warm water
   b) machine washing
   c) drying
   d) dry cleaning

166. Carolyn has finished washing and drying this piece of clothing. What should she not do now?

   a) fold it
   b) put it away
   c) wear it
   d) iron it

Go on to the next page.

DEPARTMENT OF HEALTH AND HUMAN SERVICES SOCIAL SECURITY ADMINISTRATION		Form Approved OMB No. 0960-0066

FORM SS-5 — APPLICATION FOR A SOCIAL SECURITY NUMBER CARD
(Original, Replacement or Correction)

MICROFILM REF. NO. (SSA USE ONLY)

Unless the requested information is provided, we may not be able to issue a Social Security Number (20 CFR 422.103(b))

INSTRUCTIONS TO APPLICANT	▶ Before completing this form, please read the instructions on the opposite page. You can type or print, using pen with dark blue or black ink. Do not use pencil.		
NAA NAME TO BE SHOWN ON CARD	First	Middle	Last
NAB FULL NAME AT BIRTH (IF OTHER THAN ABOVE) **1**	First	Middle	Last
ONA OTHER NAME(S) USED			
STT MAILING ADDRESS **2**	(Street/Apt. No., P.O. Box, Rural Route No.)		
CTY STE ZIP CITY		STATE	ZIP CODE

CSP CITIZENSHIP (Check one only) **3**	**SEX 4**	**SEX ETB 5**	**RACE/ETHNIC DESCRIPTION** (Check one only) (Voluntary)
☐ a U.S. citizen	☐ Male		☐ a Asian, Asian-American or Pacific Islander (Includes persons of Chinese, Filipino, Japanese, Korean, Samoan, etc., ancestry or descent)
☐ b. Legal alien allowed to work	☐ Female		☐ b Hispanic (Includes persons of Chicano, Cuban, Mexican or Mexican-American, Puerto Rican, South or Central American, or other Spanish ancestry or descent)
☐ c. Legal alien not allowed to work			☐ c Negro or Black (not Hispanic)
☐ d. Other (See instructions on Page 2)			☐ d North American Indian or Alaskan Native
			☐ e White (not Hispanic)

DOB 6 DATE OF BIRTH ▶	MONTH	DAY	YEAR	AGE **7**	PRESENT AGE	PLB **8**	PLACE OF BIRTH ▶	CITY	STATE OR FOREIGN COUNTRY
MNA 9 MOTHER'S NAME AT HER BIRTH	First							Middle	Last (her maiden name)
FNA FATHER'S NAME	First							Middle	Last

PNO a. Have you or someone on your behalf applied for a social security number before?	☐ No	☐ Don't Know	☐ Yes

Mark Martin Jenkins was born on March 28, 1965, in Denver, Colorado. His father's name is Adam Benjamin Jenkins. His mother's name is Rachel Lauren O'Brien Jenkins. He lives at 6513 S. Bellwood Place, Chicago, Illinois 60616.

167. What answer would Mark give for the first line of question 1?

   a) Mark Jenkins
   b) Mark Martin Jenkins
   c) Adam B. Jenkins
   d) R. L. Jenkins

168. What answer would Mark give for question 6?

   a) the date of the day he fills in the form
   b) Chicago, Illinois
   c) the date he receives his card
   d) March 28, 1965

169. What answer should Mark give for the first line of question 9?

   a) Rachel Jenkins
   b) Rachel Lauren Jenkins
   c) Rachel Lauren O'Brien
   d) Rachel O'Brien

170. What answer should Mark give for question 8?

   a) 60616
   b) Chicago, Illinois
   c) 6513 S. Bellwood Place
   d) Denver, Colorado

Go on to the next page.

Use the driver's license below to answer questions 171 to 174.

DRIVER'S LICENSE (Back Side)

RESTRICTION CODES
1. CORRECTIVE EYE LENSES
2. LEFT OUTSIDE MIRROR
3. DAYLIGHT DRIVING ONLY
4. AUTOMATIC TRANSMISSION
5. BUILT UP SEAT CUSHION
   OR POWER SEAT
6. OTHER — AS INDICATED

Restriction(s)	Class	Donor
2	D	Seal
3		Area

Emergency
Medical
Information
Seal
Area

Blood Type
Rh Factor **B pos.**

DRIVERS LICENSE CLASSIFICATIONS
CLASS A - ANY MOTOR VEHICLE THROUGH 8,000 LBS GROSS WEIGHT
EXCEPT CLASS L OR M
CLASS B - ANY MOTOR VEHICLE THROUGH 16,000 LBS GROSS WEIGHT
EXCEPT CLASS L OR M
CLASS C - ANY MOTOR VEHICLE EXCEPT TRUCK TRACTOR-SEMITRAILER
COMBINATIONS, STINGER STEERED SEMITRAILERS, OR CLASS
L OR M
CLASS D - ANY MOTOR VEHICLE EXCEPT CLASS L OR M
CLASS L - ONLY MOTOR DRIVEN CYCLES (LESS THAN 150 CCs)
CLASS M - ONLY MOTORCYCLES AND MOTOR DRIVEN CYCLES

171. What is the only vehicle this driver could not drive?

   a) car
   b) motorcycle
   c) truck
   d) tractor

172. What restrictions does this driver have?

   a) power seat and left outside mirror
   b) corrective lenses and left outside mirror
   c) automatic transmission and daytime driving
   d) left outside mirror and daytime driving

173. Alan received a license for a motorcycle. Which classification could he have received?

   a) D
   b) A
   c) B
   d) M

174. What is the classification of this driver's license?

   a) D
   b) 23
   c) B pos.
   d) C

Go on to the next page.

Use the advertisements below to answer questions 175 to 178.

ADVERTISEMENTS

Help Wanted

Babysitter, for 3- and 4-year-old, 3 afternoons a week, occasional evenings. References required. Call C. Hoffman, 731-1104 after 6 p.m.

Paper carrier, deliver the *Journal* every Friday. Must have a van. Call Ed Sheilds, 447-3999 9-5 only.

Salesclerk, in the gourmet food department. Experience working in store necessary. Apply in person this Tuesday at Clark's Department Store.

Teacher, for parent-run nursery school. Degree in Early Childhood Education. Send resume to Mr. Wyman at P.O. Box 15. No phone calls.

175. Which job requires that you own a van?

    a) babysitter
    b) teacher
    c) salesclerk
    d) paper carrier

176. Which job requires experience?

    a) babysitter
    b) teacher
    c) salesclerk
    d) paper carrier

177. The babysitting job requires you to work

    a) every Friday.
    b) Tuesday.
    c) holidays.
    d) 3 afternoons a week.

178. Which jobs will not allow you to apply by telephone?

    a) paper carrier and salesclerk
    b) babysitter and paper carrier
    c) salesclerk and babysitter
    d) teacher and salesclerk

Go on to the next page.

Use the ad below to answer questions 179 to 182.

CLASSIFIED ADS

For Rent

2 BR Garden APT: private patio, 2 bathrooms. Bright and spacious. Located near shopping and subway station. Call janitor at 871-1571 evenings. $525/MO.

---

179. How many bedrooms does this apartment have?

    a) 2
    b) 3
    c) 1
    d) 4

180. What would be a good time to call about this apartment?

    a) 10:00 a.m.
    b) 3:00 p.m.
    c) 12:00 p.m.
    d) 7:30 p.m.

181. According to the ad, what is convenient about this apartment's location?

    a) It is near shopping.
    b) It is private.
    c) It has a garden.
    d) It has a janitor.

182. What is the monthly rent for this apartment?

    a) $871
    b) $525
    c) $157
    d) $1,050

Go on to the next page.

Use the ad below to answer questions 183 and 184.

ADVERTISEMENT

HOLIDAY SPECIAL

The Napoleon Grandfather Clock
the finest French clock, solid oak

          Reg. $5000   sale $3850

German cuckoo clocks
made of maple veneers

          $10.50 - $55.36

small alarm clocks
blue, red, black

          $3.50 - $10.50

---

183. What is the regular price of the grandfather
clock?

    a) $5,000
    b) $3,850
    c) $55.36
    d) $10.50

184. How much is the most expensive alarm clock?

    a) $10.50
    b) $55.36
    c) $3.50
    d) $38.50

Go on to the next page.

Use the schedule below to answer questions 185 to 188.

Departs from	Train Number	Departure Time	Arrival in New York
Buffalo	112	6:00 a.m.	12:00 p.m.
Toronto	534	5:00 p.m.	8:00 a.m.
New Orleans	771	7:45 a.m.	1:00 p.m.
Dallas	986	1:00 p.m.	10:00 a.m.
Denver	671	7:00 p.m.	2:00 p.m.
Seattle	650	8:00 a.m.	9:00 p.m.
Bangor	224	11:00 a.m.	9:00 p.m.

185. Which city has the train that leaves the latest in the evening?

   a) Dallas
   b) Seattle
   c) Buffalo
   d) Denver

186. Which two trains arrive in New York at the same time?

   a) #771 and #986
   b) #650 and #112
   c) #650 and #224
   d) #534 and #650

187. Which train leaves at 5:00 p.m. and arrives in New York at 8:00 a.m.?

   a) #671
   b) #650
   c) #112
   d) #534

188. What time does the Bangor train arrive in New York?

   a) 11:00 p.m.
   b) 9:00 a.m.
   c) 11:00 a.m.
   d) 9:00 p.m.

Go on to the next page.

58

Use the program listing below to answer questions 189 to 192.

Afternoon

12:00 [2] **Noon Talk** Guest: Anna Maglen, singer

[4] **News**

[5] **News**

[7] **Movie** "Run For Your Life" (see Movie Guide)

12:30 [2] **The Stock Market**

[5] **Robert Canon** An interview with Senator Rich

1:00 [2] **Cartoons**

[4] **Life with Connie** (comedy) Connie plays a trick on Mrs. Bonner.

[5] **The Day's Events**

1:30 [7] **Afternoon Break**

---

189. What time would you turn on the set to learn about stocks?

a) 12:00
b) 12:30
c) 1:00
d) 1:30

190. What two stations have news at 12:00?

a) 2 and 7
b) 4 and 5
c) 4 and 7
d) 2 and 5

191. What time does the 12:00 movie end?

a) 12:30
b) 1:00
c) 1:30
d) 12:00

192. What time should you turn on the set to see a funny show?

a) 12:00
b) 1:30
c) 1:00
d) 12:30

Go on to the next page.

Use the phone book entries below to answer questions 193 to 196.

WHITE PAGES

P & G Decorating 715 Lake. 366-1005
Pace, Angelo 445 Ridgeland Ave 848-5764
Pace Collection Co 133 North Blvd. . . 366-7750
Pace, John 1577 N Taylor. 848-1773
Pacer, Fred D 115 Madison 771-9114
Pacer, Fred Q 113 N Addison 773-1152
Paddock, Anne 437 S Monroe 848-4944

193. What is the telephone number of the John Pace family?

   a) 771-9114
   b) 848-1773
   c) 773-1152
   d) 366-7750

194. What is the address of Fred D. Pacer?

   a) 115 Madison
   b) 113 N. Addison
   c) 1577 N. Taylor
   d) 437 S. Monroe

195. Where is P & G Decorating located?

   a) 445 Ridgeland Ave.
   b) 715 Lake
   c) 133 North Blvd.
   d) 1577 N. Taylor

196. What is the telephone number of Ms. Anne Paddock?

   a) 771-9114
   b) 773-1152
   c) 848-4944
   d) 366-7750

Go on to the next page.

Use the phone book entries below to answer questions 197 to 200.

YELLOW PAGES

▶ **Draperies and Curtains**

MAJESTIC SLIP COVER
    7134 W Jefferson 753-1234
Morris Custom Curtains
    504 N Western 667-9864
Near Beauty Interiors
    3112 E Kevin 667-1100
WINDOW WONDERS
    987 S 37th St 948-2371
Window Shades
    17 Raisin 948-1134

▶ **Dressmakers**

Lucille's Sewing Shop
    559 W Vincent 331-0198
LYMAN CUSTOM STITCHES
    19 Elm 132-1230

▶ **Driving Instruction**

Abbott Driving School
    1000 Lester 565-3222
Bennetts' Perfect Drivers
    33 Mission 431-9876

▶ **Drug Stores**
    (See Pharmacies)

▶ **Dry Cleaners**
    (See Cleaners)

197. What is the address of Window Wonders?
   a) 3112 E. Kevin
   b) 987 S. 37th St.
   c) 504 N. Western
   d) 17 Raisin

198. What is the telephone number of Abbott Driving School?
   a) 565-3222
   b) 431-9876
   c) 132-1230
   d) 948-2371

199. What heading would you look up to find a drug store?
   a) drugs
   b) cleaners
   c) pharmacies
   d) stores

200. What is the telephone number of Lyman Custom Stitches?
   a) 431-9876
   b) 331-0198
   c) 565-3222
   d) 132-1230

Form A

1. d	6. c	11. c	16. a	21. d	26. d
2. b	7. a	12. a	17. b	22. a	27. d
3. a	8. c	13. a	18. c	23. c	28. d
4. b	9. a	14. c	19. a	24. b	29. b
5. a	10. d	15. c	20. b	25. b	30. c

	incorrect	correct		incorrect	correct		incorrect	correct
31. b	nieghbor	neighbor	38. c	orginal	original	45. b	registared	registered
32. d	dimond	diamond	39. a	blizard	blizzard	46. a	comfortible	comfortable
33. d	lunchon	luncheon	40. b	guaranted	guaranteed	47. a	ocassions	occasions
34. a	marrage	marriage	41. c	aquainted	acquainted	48. c	desparate	desperate
35. b	sleaves	sleeves	42. c	citys	cities	49. b	managment	management
36. d	arguement	argument	43. b	paino	piano	50. d	visiters	visitors
37. a	asortment	assortment	44. d	neice	niece			

51. b	incorrect:	The wind blew Bens mittens down the street.
	correct:	The wind blew Ben's mittens down the street.
52. c	incorrect:	Celia collects rocks shells, and butterflies.
	correct:	Celia collects rocks, shells, and butterflies.
53. a	incorrect:	The book was too difficult for we students.
	correct:	The book was too difficult for us students.
54. c	incorrect:	Winston doesn't play the french horn very well.
	correct:	Winston doesn't play the French horn very well.
55. c	incorrect:	Yesterday Carla said, I may be late for school on Thursday."
	correct:	Yesterday Carla said, "I may be late for school on Thursday."
56. b	incorrect:	One of my favorite countries are Mexico.
	correct:	One of my favorite countries is Mexico.
57. b	incorrect:	I don't want to go to the museum no more.
	correct:	I don't want to go to the museum any more.
58. d	No mistakes.	
59. a	incorrect:	The purple collage was the better in the exhibit.
	correct:	The purple collage was the best in the exhibit.
60. a	incorrect:	Were going skiing and sledding when the weather turns cold.
	correct:	We're going skiing and sledding when the weather turns cold.
61. a	incorrect:	Kim and me are the best of friends.
	correct:	Kim and I are the best of friends.
62. b	incorrect:	Sally asked, "when are we visiting the cranberry factory?"
	correct:	Sally asked, "When are we visiting the cranberry factory?"
63. b	incorrect:	After we finish lunch, we went to the swimming pool.
	correct:	After we finished lunch, we went to the swimming pool.
	or:	After we finish lunch, we will go to the swimming pool.
64. c	incorrect:	He addressed the book about languages to j. r. evans.
	correct:	He addressed the book about languages to J. R. Evans.
65. c	incorrect:	Pat have driven to the airport to pick up her grandmother.
	correct:	Pat has driven to the airport to pick up her grandmother.
	or:	Pat had driven to the airport to pick up her grandmother.

66. b incorrect: Silver necklaces were given to she and I.
      correct: Silver necklaces were given to her and me.
67. b incorrect: Washington Irving wrote many fine books and tales such as "the legend of sleepy hollow."
      correct: Washington Irving wrote many fine books and tales such as "The Legend of Sleepy Hollow."
68. b incorrect: The new foreign students will arrive on monday by ship.
      correct: The new foreign students will arrive on Monday by ship.
69. a incorrect: Carol and Sara swum thirty laps in the pool.
      correct: Carol and Sara swam thirty laps in the pool.
70. c incorrect: Tulips are beautiful flowers because of they're color.
      correct: Tulips are beautiful flowers because of their color.
71. a incorrect: The race began at Lawrence ave., continued down the road along the river, and finished at the elementary school.
      correct: The race began at Lawrence Ave., continued down the road along the river, and finished at the elementary school.
72. d No mistakes.
73. c incorrect: Why don't you leave your cat with us Frances asked.
      correct: "Why don't you leave your cat with us?" Frances asked.
74. d No mistakes.
75. b incorrect: Us and them have tickets for tonight's game.
      correct: We and they have tickets for tonight's game.
76. c incorrect: "What a beautiful star," Marie exclaimed.
      correct: "What a beautiful star!" Marie exclaimed.
77. a incorrect: My friend's two older brothers are Doctors.
      correct: My friend's two older brothers are doctors.
78. c incorrect: Ever since we were in third grade, he and I, have been best friends.
      correct: Ever since we were in third grade, he and I have been best friends.
79. a incorrect: Henrik Ibsen wrote the play "the wild duck."
      correct: Henrik Ibsen wrote the play "The Wild Duck."
80. d No mistakes.
81. c incorrect: I are visiting relatives in Greece next summer.
      correct: I am visiting relatives in Greece next summer.
82. a incorrect: She said, "we will be camping in Canada soon."
      correct: She said, "We will be camping in Canada soon."
83. c incorrect: Peter made his bed dusted his dresser and picked up his clothes before he left for the movies.
      correct: Peter made his bed, dusted his dresser, and picked up his clothes before he left for the movies.
84. a incorrect: "Ain't this exciting?" asked Bobby.
      correct: "Isn't this exciting?" asked Bobby.
85. a incorrect: That foreign student speaks English good.
      correct: That foreign student speaks English well.
86. a incorrect: The north and the south fought in the Civil War.
      correct: The North and the South fought in the Civil War.
87. b incorrect: Each of the musicians were pleased with the performance.
      correct: Each of the musicians was pleased with the performance.
88. c incorrect: I have lend that to you before.
      correct: I have lent that to you before.

89. b incorrect: We haven't never been there before.
       correct: We have never been there before.
       or: We haven't ever been there before.
90. b incorrect: Doesn't those pictures need to be framed for the holidays?
       correct: Don't those pictures need to be framed for the holidays?
       or: Doesn't that picture need to be framed for the holidays?

91. d	121. a	151. b	181. a
92. c	122. a	152. a	182. b
93. b	123. a	153. a	183. a
94. b	124. c	154. d	184. a
95. b	125. a	155. d	185. d
96. d	126. a	156. b	186. c
97. b	127. d	157. d	187. d
98. d	128. b	158. d	188. d
99. b	129. d	159. d	189. b
100. a	130. d	160. c	190. b
101. c	131. b	161. a	191. c
102. c	132. d	162. b	192. c
103. c	133. c	163. a	193. b
104. d	134. d	164. d	194. a
105. a	135. b	165. d	195. b
106. c	136. a	166. d	196. c
107. c	137. b	167. b	197. b
108. d	138. a	168. d	198. a
109. d	139. c	169. c	199. c
110. d	140. a	170. d	200. d
111. a	141. c	171. b	
112. b	142. a	172. d	
113. a	143. b	173. d	
114. b	144. c	174. a	
115. a	145. c	175. d	
116. a	146. c	176. c	
117. a	147. d	177. d	
118. c	148. b	178. d	
119. c	149. b	179. a	
120. c	150. a	180. d	

Objectives	Item Numbers
I. LANGUAGE SKILLS	
A. Vocabulary	1, 2, 3, 4, 5, 6, 7, 8, 9, 10, 11, 12, 13, 14, 15, 16, 17, 18, 19, 20, 21, 22, 23, 24, 25, 26, 27, 28, 29, 30
B. Spelling	31, 32, 33, 34, 35, 36, 37, 38, 39, 40, 41, 42, 43, 44, 45, 46, 47, 48, 49, 50
C. Writing Skills	
1. Capitalization	54, 62, 64, 67, 68, 71, 77, 79, 82, 86
2. Punctuation	51, 52, 55, 58, 60, 72, 73, 76, 78, 83
3. Grammar	53, 56, 57, 59, 61, 63, 65, 66, 69, 70, 74, 75, 80, 81, 84, 85, 87, 88, 89, 90
II. READING SKILLS	
A. Literal Comprehension	92, 93, 95, 96, 101, 102, 104, 105, 108, 109, 111, 113, 117, 119, 120, 121
B. Inferential Comprehension	91, 94, 97, 98, 99, 100, 103, 106, 107, 110, 112, 114, 115, 116, 118, 122
III. REFERENCE SKILLS	
A. Alphabetical Order	123, 124, 125, 126
B. Following Directions	127, 128, 129, 130
C. Table of Contents	131, 132, 133, 134
D. Reference Sources	135, 136, 137, 138, 139, 140, 141, 142
E. Dictionary Entry	143, 144, 145, 146
F. Book Index	147, 148, 149, 150

Objectives	Item Numbers
G. Maps	
1. Street Maps	151, 152, 153, 154
2. Highway Maps	155, 156, 157, 158
IV. LIFE SKILLS	
A. Labels	
1. Medicine Bottle Labels	159, 160, 161, 162
2. Clothing Labels	163, 164, 165, 166
B. Forms	
1. Social Security Application	167, 168, 169, 170
2. Driver's License	171, 172, 173, 174
C. Advertisements	
1. Help Wanted	175, 176, 177, 178
2. For Rent	179, 180, 181, 182
3. Product Ads	183, 184
D. Schedules	
1. Train Schedule	185, 186, 187, 188
2. TV Schedule	189, 190, 191, 192
E. Telephone Book	
1. White Pages	193, 194, 195, 196
2. Yellow Pages	197, 198, 199, 200

I. LANGUAGE SKILLS

Language skills include vocabulary, spelling, and writing skills. They are necessary for developing good communication skills.

A. Vocabulary

It is important to expand your vocabulary to include as many words as possible. The way a word is used can often help you to better understand it.

For example, you may not know the meaning of the word *synthetic* but you might understand it by reading the sentences "This fabric is synthetic; it contains only man-made materials," or "This juice contains no natural flavors; it is synthetically flavored." Using a dictionary to look up unfamiliar words and using a thesaurus to find synonyms and antonyms can increase your vocabulary.

B. Spelling

Proper spelling helps you learn how to pronounce words and understand what you read. Again, using a dictionary can help improve your spelling skills.

For example, you may not know the spelling of a word. You have looked up some possibilities, but find that none of them are correct. Now look at the pronunciation key at the front of the dictionary. You will discover how certain sounds are spelled and how certain letter combinations are pronounced. Then you should be able to find the correct spelling of a word. On the next page is a sample pronunciation key.

SAMPLE PRONUNCIATION KEY

a	add, cat, carry		o	on, fox, watch
ā	ache, ape, say		ō	open, coat, know
â(r)	air, care, Larry		ô	bought, fall, saw
ä	all, part, palm		oi	foil, join, boy
b	bat, cable, nab		o͝o	cook, floor
ch	cheat, pitcher, peach		o͞o	loose, cool, moo
d	due, redder, head		ou	our, cloud, brow
e	web, net, berry		p	pit, stopper, tap
ē	even, seal, beet, nightly		r	reed, flurry, dear
ēr	fear, mere		s	seed, missing, class
f	first, differ, muff		sh	ship, cushion, rush
g	gift, bigger, leg		t	tan, bitter, pit
h	him, haven, here		th	thick, northern, pith
hw	while, nowhere		t͟h	then, neither, sooth
i	in, dig, cirrus, publish		u	us, dove
ī	icon, site, siren, reply		û(r)	urn, turn, fur
j	jug, gadget, judge		v	vest, liver, love
k	keg, poker, lake		w	waste, awake
l	lob, yellow, call		y	yet, lawyer
m	mine, summer, hum		z	zest, hazy, chase
n	no, thinner, don		zh	pleasure, garage
ng	ring, Washington		ə	a in along
				e in sister
				i in feasible
				o in wallop
				u in conquer

C. **Writing Skills**

1. **Capitalization**

You should be able to recognize that the following items require capitalization:

- proper nouns

    names of people, pets, holidays, days of the week, months, towns, cities, states, streets, initials, or personal titles

    Example:

    > On Monday, Jane will visit Dr. McIntyre.

    not   On monday, jane will visit dr. mcintyre.

    > On St. Patrick's Day, there is a parade down State Street.

    not   On st. patrick's day, there is a parade down state street.

    names of countries, geographical locations, important structures, or companies

    Example:

    > The Sears Tower is the tallest building in the Midwest.

    not   The sears tower is the tallest building in the midwest.

    > The Nestle Company is based in Switzerland.

    not   The nestle company is based in switzerland.

names of schools, nationalities, languages, products, or special events

Example:

> That Briton also speaks German and French.

not   That briton also speaks german and french.

> The Chicago Fire happened in 1871.

not   The chicago fire happened in 1871.

- important words in the title of a book, play, or article

Example:

> I enjoyed reading The Old Man and the Sea.

not   I enjoyed reading the old man and the sea.

> Edgar Allan Poe wrote "The Fall of the House of Usher."

not   Edgar Allan Poe wrote "the fall of the house of usher."

- abbreviations for names of streets, states, cities, countries, months, days of the week, organizations, or titles

Example:

> Lincoln Ave. leads to the central YMCA.

not   Lincoln ave. leads to the central ymca.

> Dr. Gross has offices in White Plains, N.Y., and Greenwich, Conn.

not   Dr. Gross has offices in white plains, n.y., and greenwich, conn.

- proper adjectives

  Example

	He is as all-American as apple pie.
not	He is as all-american as apple pie.
	Shakespeare lived in Elizabethan times.
not	Shakespeare lived in elizabethan times.

- the first word of a direct quote

  Example:

	He said, "Let's go to a movie."
not	He said, "let's go to a movie."
	The newscaster said, "The price of gold fell today."
not	The newscaster said, "the price of gold fell today."

2. **Punctuation**

You should be able to recognize the following punctuation requirements:

- commas

  commas should be used to separate items in a series

  Example:

	We bought apples, bananas, raisins, and strawberries.
not	We bought apples bananas raisins and strawberries.

Birds, kites, airplanes, and bees can fly.

not   Birds kites airplanes and bees can fly.

a comma should be used before *and*, *or*, and *but* in a compound sentence

Example:

I called yesterday, but there was no answer.

not   I called yesterday but there was no answer.

He is jogging, and she is playing racquetball.

not   He is jogging and she is playing racquetball.

a comma separates street from city, city from state, day of the week from month, or day of the month from year

Example:

They live at 129 Birch, San Jose, California.

not   They live at 129 Birch San Jose California.

He was born on Monday, April 4, 1977.

not   He was born on Monday April 4 1977.

a comma should be used in direct address and after exclamatory words

Example:

Here is a note for you, Jim.

not   Here is a note for you Jim.

Wow, that was a great catch!

not   Wow that was a great catch!

commas should be used to set off appositives and paren-thetical expressions

Example:

Morgan, our new dog, is a terrier.

not   Morgan our new dog is a terrier.

Try the diet for, say, a week.

not   Try the diet for say a week.

a comma should be used after an introductory participial phrase or adverbial clause

Example:

Driving a car, a person must be careful.

not   Driving a car a person must be careful.

After the sun goes down, the temperature is cooler.

not   After the sun goes down the temperature is cooler.

a comma should be used after an introductory infinitive phrase or a series of prepositional phrases

Example:

To keep warm, they wrapped themselves in blankets.

not   To keep warm they wrapped themselves in blankets.

Behind the box on the left, John found
an empty bin.

not   Behind the box on the left John found
an empty bin.

- an exclamatory sentence should end with an exclamation
mark

Example:

Watch out for that truck!

not   Watch out for that truck.

- an apostrophe should be used in a contraction and to show
possession

Example:

He hasn't seen that movie.

not   He hasnt seen that movie.

The girls' team won the finals.

not   The girls team won the finals.

- quotation marks should be used to set off direct quotations
and titles of short works

Example:

"It's a surprise," she said.

not   It's a surprise, she said.

"Rip Van Winkle" is a good story.

not   Rip Van Winkle is a good story.

- a colon should be used when expressing the time of day in numerals or when introducing a series

Example:

> The plane will land at 3:55 p.m.
>
> The following tools are needed: a hammer, nails, screws, and a screwdriver.
>
> not   The following tools are needed a hammer, nails, screws, and a screwdriver.

- the title of a book or movie should be underlined

Example:

> Star Wars is a very popular movie.
>
> Treasure Island is an exciting book.

- a hyphen should be used to join words of a written numeral or compound word modifiers

Example:

> This house is seventy-four years old.
>
> The red-haired boy is cute.

- a semicolon should be used to separate clauses with no expressed connective

Example:

> The invitation came too late; the party was yesterday.
>
> not   The invitation came too late the party was yesterday.

3. **Grammar**

Make sure you understand these topics:

- verbs

recognize the correct past tense form of an irregular verb

Example:

	present tense	past tense
	I write	I wrote
	I sing	I sang
	I teach	I taught
not		I writed
		I singed
		I teached

recognize the correct auxiliaries (modals or helping verbs)

Example:

It could have been true.

not   It could of been true.

It might have been so.

not   It might of been so.

recognize the correct form of a verb that is frequently misused

Example:

Can you lend me $5?

not   Can you loan me $5?

> ₩ Sit still and stop complaining.

> not   Set still and stop complaining.

- pronouns

recognize the correct pronoun case

nominative — pronoun used as a subject

   I, he, she, it, we, they, you (singular and plural)

objective — pronoun used as an object

   me, him, her, it, us, them, you (singular and plural)

possessive — pronoun which possesses something

   my, mine, his, hers, its, our, ours, their, theirs, your and yours (singular and plural)

Example:

>   nominative — <u>I</u> have a red bicycle.

>   objective — That red bicycle belongs to <u>me</u>.

>   possessive — That red bicycle is <u>mine</u>.

If there is a double subject or a double object, both pronouns must be in the same case.

Example:

>   double subject (nominative)

>   <u>He and I</u> are going to the library.

>   double object (objective)

>   The playoff was between <u>us and them</u>.

- recognize the appropriate word needed to avoid using a double negative

Example:

There isn't anything I can do about it.

not   There isn't nothing I can do about it.

They haven't been here before.

not   They haven't never been here before.

- subject-verb agreement

singular subjects take singular verbs and plural subjects take plural verbs

Example:

She has won the lottery.

not   She have won the lottery.

They eat out once a week.

not   They eats out once a week.

a verb with a contraction must agree with the subject

Example:

They haven't any money.

not   They hasn't any money.

He isn't here.

not   He aren't here.

when the subject and its modifier are not of the same number, the verb must still agree with the subject

Example:

> One of these records is yours.

not   One of these records are yours.

> Each of the children has chores to do.

not   Each of the children have chores to do.

- recognize homonyms and know their meanings

some common homonyms you should be able to identify (check your dictionary if you are unsure):

break	brake	
who's	whose	
past	passed	
minor	miner	
waste	waist	
their	there	they're
principle	principal	
peace	piece	
capitol	capital	
plain	plane	
course	coarse	
to	too	two

● know the proper comparative or superlative adjective (again, check your dictionary if you are not sure):

comparative endings are -er, -ier, or using the word *more*; use the comparative when comparing two.

superlative endings are -est, -iest, or using the word *most*; use the superlative when comparing three or more.

Example:

	comparative	superlative
soft	softer	softest
easy	easier	easiest
pleased	more pleased	most pleased

some irregular forms are:

	comparative	superlative
bad	worse	worst
good	better	best
many	more	most

II. READING SKILLS

A. Literal Comprehension

Literal comprehension means understanding what you have read and being able to recall details mentioned in the material you have read.

Example:

Mother's Day and Father's Day are both celebrated in December in Yugoslavia. Children playfully tie up their mother or father. The captured parent must give each child a small present. Then the parent is untied, and a celebration follows.

Questions that check for literal comprehension could be as follows:

1. In what month is Mother's Day celebrated in Yugoslavia?

2. In what country is Father's Day celebrated in December?

3. Who gives the presents?

4. Who is tied up?

The answers to each of these questions can be found in the story, though perhaps in different words. Remember, literal comprehension requires you to recall facts.

B. **Inferential Comprehension**

Inferential comprehension means understanding what you have read and being able to infer, or draw conclusions, based on the material you have read.

Example:

A poor toll-gatherer and his family lived in a house on a bridge. A stormy winter caused the river to overflow, and now it seemed the bridge was about to collapse. As the family cried out for help, a rich nobleman offered two hundred gold pieces to anyone who would save them. Although many onlookers felt sorry for the poor family, none tried to help them. Suddenly, a peasant jumped in a boat and rescued the family. Minutes later the bridge and the house were swept away. Everyone cheered for the peasant, but he would not accept the gold. Instead, he gave it to the toll-gatherer and his family.

Questions that check for inferential comprehension could be as follows:

1. The bridge was probably made of

   *a) wood.
     b) concrete.
     c) steel.
     d) iron.

2. The peasant gave the gold to the toll-gatherer and his family because

     a) he himself was rich.
   *b) they had lost everything.
     c) they asked him for it.
     d) it belonged to them.

The answers to each of these questions are conclusions drawn from the information in the story. The bridge was most likely made of wood, because wood is the least heavy of the materials listed and would be more easily swept away.

The answer to the second question, "*b,*" is the best possible choice. We know a peasant is not rich, and we know the gold belonged to the rich nobleman. The toll-gatherer was grateful to the peasant for having saved his life, and most likely would not have asked for the gold. We do know that the poor family lost everything they had, and we know that the peasant was a generous man (because he risked danger to help them), so we know "*b*" is the best answer. Remember, inferential comprehension requires you to draw conclusions from what you have read.

III. REFERENCE SKILLS

A. Alphabetical Order

Recognizing alphabetical order is a skill you need to know when looking things up in a telephone directory, a file system, a book index, an encyclopedia, a dictionary, and other sources.

Example:

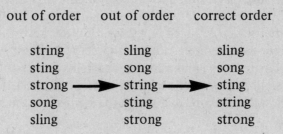

out of order	out of order	correct order
string	sling	sling
sting	song	song
strong	string	sting
song	sting	string
sling	strong	strong

To put words in alphabetical order, you begin by looking at the first letter of each word. If they are all the same, look at the second letter, if the first and second are all the same, look at the third letter, etc. When you find a place where the letters are not all the same, arrange the words alphabetically by that letter position. Continue doing this until the entire list of words is arranged alphabetically.

B. Following Directions

Directions tell you how to do or make things. A set of directions can tell you how to play a game, how to work on your car, how to cook a meal, how to use an appliance, or what to do in an emergency.

Example:

This set of directions tells how to use an electric coffee mill.

1. Fill with desired amount of coffee beans, but not past indicator line.
2. Place cover on unit.
3. Plug power cord into AC outlet.
4. Press button on cover and hold for 30 seconds.
5. Unplug unit before removing ground coffee.

By following these steps, you can be sure that you are using the appliance correctly and safely. When interpreting directions, make sure that you follow the exact order of steps (example, put the cover on *before* plugging in the cord), and make sure that you understand the directions exactly (hold button for 30 seconds, not 50 and not 10).

C. Table of Contents

Books and magazines have a table of contents that tells you what can be found and on what page it can be found. The items in the list are usually arranged in numerical order according to the page number. For example, a novel's table of contents will list the chapters by name and number, and tell you what page each chapter starts on. A magazine's table of contents will list the names of the articles, the authors, and the page numbers of the articles.

Example:

Looking at the table of contents, you can see that Chapter 2 starts on page 24 and that prepositions are discussed on page 19. You will also notice that the table is arranged numerically, in order by page number.

D.   Reference Sources

Reference sources include the following: dictionary, thesaurus, encyclopedia, atlas, almanac, glossary, index, table of contents, library card catalog, and *Guinness Book of World Records*.

Reference sources can provide you with unlimited information and are quite useful. Study the list below and become familiar with the sources, the types of information they contain, and how to use them.

source	type of information
card catalog	a file in alphabetical order which lists the items in a library, identified by author, title, or subject
dictionary	a book with words of a language in alphabetic order, with information about their meanings, pronunciations, spellings, origins, etc.
atlas	a collection of maps (of countries, roads, etc.)
almanac	an annual publication with useful and interesting facts about a variety of subjects; a list of events and times for sunrises, eclipses, any other phenomena for the upcoming year; statistical data, etc.

source	type of information
thesaurus	a dictionary of synonyms and antonyms
encyclopedia	a volume of books containing information about a variety of subjects in all branches of knowledge, arranged alphabetically
Guinness Book of World Records	a book containing information about various world records, such as who set them and when

Example:

> Which reference source would you
> use to find out the origin of the word
> *chauffeur*?
>
> a) encyclopedia
> b) thesaurus
> *c) dictionary
> d) card catalog

By checking the list of sources, you will see that a dictionary tells about the origin of a word, so *c* is the correct answer.

> Which reference source would you
> use to find out the average size of
> a farm in the United States?
>
> a) *Guinness Book of World Records*
> *b) almanac
> c) encyclopedia
> d) card catalog

Again, by checking the list of sources and becoming familiar with the items, you will be able to find the answer in an almanac.

E. Dictionary Entry

From a dictionary entry you can determine the spelling of a word, its meaning, how to pronounce it, and what part of speech it is. Sometimes synonyms, antonyms, or the origin of a word are given. Sometimes sample sentences are given, to show you how to use a word.

Example:

> **fla·vor** (flā′ vər), *n.* **1.** taste, esp. the distinctive taste of something as it is experienced in the mouth. **2.** a substance that provides a particular flavor. —*v.t.* **3.** to give flavor to (something). —**syn. 1.** See **taste. 3.** essence, spirit.

From the sample you can see that *flavor* has two syllables, with the accent on the first syllable. The **boldface** numbers indicate different meanings or uses of the word. There are three definitions listed above. The letter or letters in *italics* indicate what part of speech the word is. Flavor is a noun *(n.)* when used with the meaning of definition 1 or 2, and a transitive verb *(v.t.)* when used with the meaning of definition 3. A synonym for the first definition of flavor is taste, and synonyms for the third definition of flavor are essence and spirit. The origin of flavor is not given here.

F. Book Index

A book index is an alphabetical listing of the topics covered in a book and the page(s) on which they can be found.

Example:

Index	
Afghans.	75, 76
Counted Cross-stitch	36, 37, 39
Crewel Embroidery	28-35
Crocheting.	67-74
Knitting.	61-66
Latch Hooking	43, 44
Needlepoint.	21-28
Quilting.	77-81
Sewing.	96-109
Tapestries	81, 82-85

From the sample index you can see that information about quilting is on pages 77 through 81, afghans are discussed on pages 75 and 76, and counted cross-stitch is covered on pages 36, 37, and 39. The alphabetical order makes the index easy to use.

G. Maps

1. Street Maps

Most people will have to read a map at some time, especially those who travel or move often. Learning to read a map is not too difficult and is a good skill to acquire.

Example:

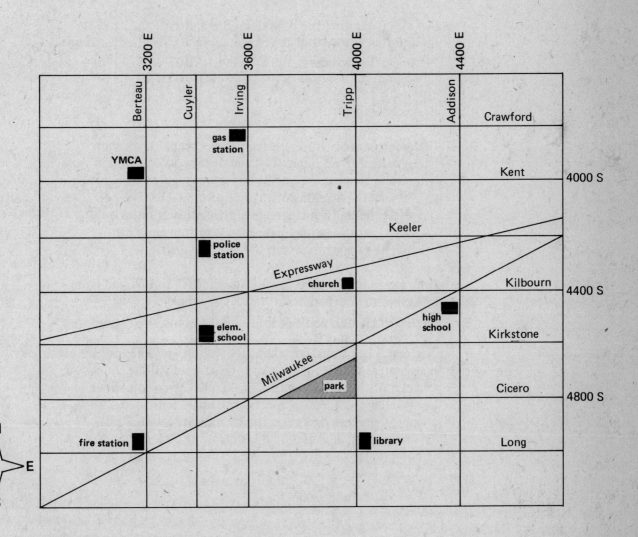

A map will have a direction key to indicate which direction is north, south, east, or west. All major streets will be labeled, and sometimes minor streets will also be labeled. Places of interest or importance, such as police stations, hospitals, museums, schools, etc. will be marked. Expressways will also be shown.

Look at the sample street map, and you can see that a church is located at Tripp and Kilbourn, which is 4000 E and 4400 S. You can also see that Addison runs in a north-south direction and Crawford runs in an east-west direction.

See if you can find the police and fire stations, the park, the library, the YMCA, and the two schools. As you find each one, name the street it is on, the direction of the street, and the nearest street that runs in the opposite direction.

2. **Highway Maps**

Highway maps are different from street maps. They show cities, towns, roads, highways, and distances. Some maps will also show places of major importance, such as colleges, airports, state parks, historical monuments, etc. They do not show the individual streets in the towns or cities on the map itself, but they may have insets for the major cities showing the major streets in the business districts.

Highway maps are used to determine which routes lead from one place to another, and are necessary for drivers who are leaving town for a particular destination.

The map's key indicates what the symbols and lines on the map represent. Each particular type of road will be shown in a certain way; this can be a broken line, two solid lines, a particular color, etc. Airports are usually indicated with a plane, and state parks are usually indicated with a tree. The mileage is indicated by a scale.

Example:

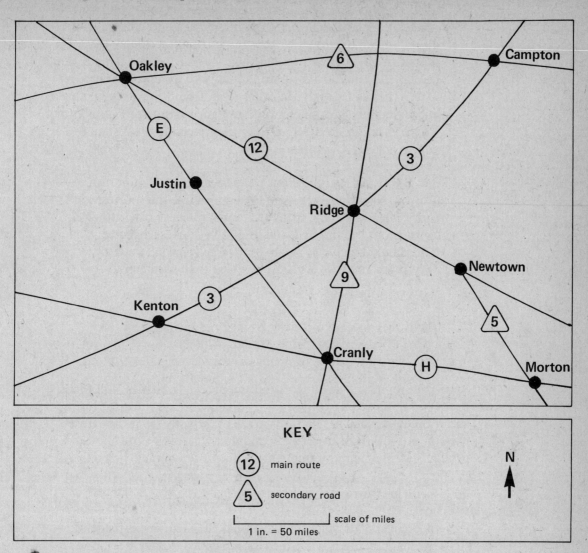

KEY

⑫ main route

△5 secondary road

⊢————⊣ scale of miles
1 in. = 50 miles

N
↑

By studying the sample road map and its key, you will notice the different ways of indicating main routes and secondary roads. You will also notice that in some cases you may go directly from one town to another, but that in other cases, you must first go to one town and then the other. For example, you can take Route 3 from Kenton directly to Campton, approximately 225 miles away. In order to go from Kenton to Oakley, approximately 125 miles away, you must first take Route 3 to Route E, and then Route E to Oakley, making the distance approximately 185 miles.

See if you can find different ways to get from Campton to Morton, Newtown, or Justin, and determine the shortest route. Then try going from each town to every other town, figuring out the mileage, and using the shortest distance. You should be able to figure out the mileage between any two towns and the direction in which each road runs.

IV. LIFE SKILLS

A. Labels

Labels are found on clothing, furniture, medicine bottles, and food products, among other things. They usually contain information about the item, such as what it is made of, how to use it, how to clean it, etc. Learn to read labels, and you will learn more about products with which you frequently come into contact.

1. Medicine Bottle Labels

Medicine bottle labels tell you what the medicine is made of, the manufacturer, what the recommended dosage is, who may or may not use the medicine, the intended result of using it, any possible side effects of using it, and what to do if it is taken by someone who shouldn't have used it or if too much is taken.

Example:

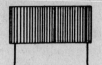

COUGH SYRUP

For temporary relief of cough-ing.

Dosage:

Adults and children over 16
2 tablespoonfuls every 3 hours; do not exceed 16 tablespoon-fuls in 24 hours.

Children over 10 yrs.
1 tablespoonful every 3 hours; do not exceed 8 tablespoonfuls in 24 hours.

Children between 2 and 10 yrs.
1 teaspoonful every 4 hours; do not exceed 6 teaspoonfuls in 24 hours. Do not administer to children under 2 yrs.

WARNING: If cough persists more than five days or condi-tion worsens, consult your physician.

From this sample medicine bottle label, you can see that the dosage varies according to the age of the person using the medicine. There are three dosages — one for children age 2-10, one for children age 10-16, and one for anyone over 16; children under 2 should not be given this medicine. You can also see that this medicine is intended only for the relief of coughing. The warning tells you under what conditions to see a doctor. By carefully reading the label before you take medicine or give it to someone else, you can avoid making a dangerous mistake.

2. **Clothing Labels**

Clothing labels usually contain the name of the manufacturer, the style number, the size, the cleaning instructions, and the materials used to make the item.

Example:

---

made by:

STITCHES, INC.

STYLE NO.:   067-531
SIZE: M

FABRIC CONTENT: ACRYLIC — 85%
                 WOOL — 15%

TO CLEAN: WASH IN COLD WATER
           LAY FLAT TO DRY
           DO NOT TUMBLE DRY
           OR WRING

From the sample label, you can see that the garment was manufactured by Stitches, Inc. You can see that the style number is 067-531, and the size is M, medium. The garment is made of 85% acrylic and 15% wool. It should be washed in cold water and dried by laying it out flat. It should not be wrung out or put in a dryer. Practice reading the labels on your clothes and some food products in your home.

B.   Forms

Quite often we are required to fill out forms — for school, work, banks, the government, businesses, etc. It is to your advantage to become familiar with commonly used forms and to learn how to fill them out.

On the next two pages are two job application forms, one blank and one filled in. Study the completed application form carefully. Then practice filling in the blank form following it. Be sure to answer all questions that apply to you. Skip those that do not (do not write in the spaces that ask about military service if you have not served in the armed forces).

Most people will have to fill out a job application at least once during their working years. The form asks for general information about you, your education, and your work experience. Remember that every blank needs to be filled in if it applies to you. Give information exactly as it is asked for, for example, last name first (not first name first) or mother's maiden name (not married name).

Application For Employment

(answer all questions - please print)

In compliance with Federal and State equal employment opportunity laws, qualified applicants are considered for all positions without regard to race, color, religion, sex, national origin, age, marital status, or the presence of a non-job-related medical condition or handicap.

Date of Application _3. 5. 82_

Position(s) Applied For _Cashier / Stock_

Referral Source ☑ Advertisement ☐ Friend ☐ Relative

☐ Employment Agency ☐ Other_____

Name _Aust_ _Tony_ _Peter_ Social Security No. _441-19-6302_
LAST FIRST MIDDLE

Address _902 S. Euclid_ _Riverton_ _IL_ _60938_
STREET CITY STATE ZIP

Phone _739-0152_ Are you known to schools/references by another name? ☐ Yes ☑ No

If yes, by what name? _____

Have you filed an application or been employed here before? ☐ Yes ☑ No Date(s) _____

Are you a Citizen of the United States? ☑ Yes ☐ No

If not, do you possess an Alien Registration Card? ☐ Yes ☐ No

Are you available to work? ☐ Full Time ☑ Part Time ☐ On Shifts

Do Any of Your Friends or Relatives Work Here? ☐ Yes ☑ No

If Yes, List Name(s) _____

Are you? ☑ Under 18 ☐ 18-70 ☐ Over 70 years of age

Have you been convicted of a felony or released from prison within the last 7 years? ☐ Yes ☑ No

If yes, describe in full, including date(s)_____

In case of accident or emergency, please notify:
Michael Aust _902 S. Euclid_ _739-0152_
NAME ADDRESS PHONE NO.

AN EQUAL EMPLOYMENT OPPORTUNITY EMPLOYER M/F

Application
For Employment

In compliance with Federal and State equal employment opportunity laws, qualified applicants are considered for all positions without regard to race, color, religion, sex, national origin, age, marital status, or the presence of a non-job-related medical condition or handicap.

Date of Application_____

Position(s) Applied For _____

Referral Source   ☐ Advertisement   ☐ Friend   ☐ Relative

                   ☐ Employment Agency   ☐ Other_____

Name _____ Social Security No._____
       LAST   FIRST   MIDDLE

Address _____
       STREET   CITY   STATE   ZIP

Phone_____Are you known to schools/references by another name? ☐ Yes   ☐ No

If yes, by what name? _____

Have you filed an application or been employed here before? ☐ Yes   ☐ No   Date(s) _____

Are you a Citizen of the United States?   ☐ Yes   ☐ No

If not, do you possess an Alien Registration Card?   ☐ Yes   ☐ No

Are you available to work?   ☐ Full Time   ☐ Part Time   ☐ On Shifts

Do Any of Your Friends or Relatives Work Here?   ☐ Yes   ☐ No

If Yes, List Name(s) _____

Are you?   ☐ Under 18   ☐ 18-70   ☐ Over 70 years of age

Have you been convicted of a felony or released from prison within the last 7 years?   ☐ Yes ☐ No

If yes, describe in full, including date(s)_____

_____

_____

In case of accident or emergency, please notify:

_____
NAME   ADDRESS   PHONE NO.

AN EQUAL EMPLOYMENT OPPORTUNITY EMPLOYER M/F

C. Advertisements

Newspapers and magazines usually contain advertisements. These
may be advertisements for help wanted (job openings), advertisements encouraging you to buy certain products, or advertisements
announcing housing for rent or sale. Advertisements are also found
on billboards and benches, in store windows, on the radio, and on
television. Classified advertisements are short advertisements usually
found in magazines or newspapers, and grouped according to type
of advertisement, such as "For Rent," "Help Wanted," "For Sale,"
etc. People place advertisements to find a lost pet, to sell a used car
or other items, to find a roommate, or to find someone to share
a ride. Businesses place advertisements for their products or for
help wanted. Advertising is an ever-present factor in our daily lives.
You should familiarize yourself with different types of advertisements and their purposes, and learn how to interpret them.

1. Help Wanted

"Help wanted" advertisements are placed by employers who are
looking for new employees. Sometimes these advertisements
contain very little information, just enough to get you interested in the job, and how to apply for it. Some "help wanted"
advertisements will also tell you about the job, the salary, the
benefits, the company that is hiring, and the qualifications for
getting the job.

Example:

TUTORS

Tutors needed with strong English
background. Help foreign business
people improve communication skills.
Contact Shannon at 281-9065.

This sample "help wanted" advertisement tells you the type of job — tutor, and one of the requirements — a strong English background. It tells you who you would be working with — foreign business people. The advertisement does not tell you the name of the company that is hiring or the salary they are offering, but it does tell you to call Shannon to find out additional information. Practice reading "help wanted" advertisements in a newspaper until you feel confident about interpreting them.

2. **For Rent**

"For rent" advertisements usually describe apartments or houses that are available to renters. Some of these advertisements may tell you only the size of the residence and a phone number to call for more details. Other "for rent" advertisements may tell you the address or general location of the residence, how much the rent is, what appliances or furnishings are included, when the residence will be available, etc. Most "for rent" advertisements contain abbreviations, so you will have to practice reading them until you know what the abbreviations stand for.

Example:

FOR RENT

5-rm apt., 3rd fl., w-w cptg., heat incl., NW loc., nr. trans., shpg., pk., schools. No pets. Call 549-8360 for appt.

This sample "for rent" advertisement provides quite a bit of information. A third-floor apartment with five rooms is available on the northwest side of the city. The apartment is near public transportation, a shopping area, a park, and schools. There is wall-to-wall carpeting in the apartment, no pets are allowed, and the heat is included in the rent. You must make an appointment to see the apartment, or you may call the number provided for additional information. Practice reading "for rent" advertisements in a newspaper until you feel confident about interpreting them.

3.   **Product Ads**

Product ads are advertisements that offer merchandise for sale. The merchandise may be a new product or an old product, it may be on sale at a reduced price, or it may be discontinued. Product ads appear in newspapers, magazines, store windows, on radio, on television, or on billboards.

Example:

SALE!

Rudy's Bike Shop
4901 W. Grace
725-0616

Ladies' and men's bicycles reduced:

		was	now
10-speed	Roadster	$399.95	$250.00
5-speed	Traveler	$299.95	$195.00
3-speed	Roundabout	$199.95	$130.00

While supplies last.

This sample product ad describes a sale on bicycles at Rudy's Bicycle Shop. The store's address and phone number are listed, so interested customers can either call or stop by. Both ladies' and men's bicycles are on sale. Three models are listed. The regular price is shown before the sale price. "While supplies last" means that only those bicycles in stock will be sold at the sale price; additional bicycles will not be ordered to be sold at the discounted rate. Practice reading product ads in magazines and newspapers.

D. Schedules

Schedules are a large factor in your daily routine. You are following a schedule at school and at work. When you travel by bus, boat, train, or airplane, you use a schedule to determine departure and arrival times, and the length of the trip. When you watch television, you use a schedule to find out what programs are on, what time they start and finish, and on what channel they are. You schedule appointments with your doctor, dentist, or mechanic, etc.

Example:

EASTERN COLLEGE

CLASS SCHEDULE

Adrian Albrecht   Term: Winter, 1982
3935 N. Kilbourn
Chicago, IL 60641   Status: Freshman
(312) 475-1409

Course		M	T	W	TH	F
14-100	Literature and Writing Rm A-115	9:00– 9:50		9:00– 9:50	9:00– 9:50	
12-110	Art in Society Rm 3-3001		10:00– 10:50		10:00– 10:50	10:00– 10:50
15-200	German II Rm LANG LAB	10:00– 11:25		10:00– 11:25		
16-200	College Algebra Rm S-112	12:00– 12:50		12:00– 12:50		12:00– 12:50
19-150	Environmental Studies Rm 2-020		11:00– 11:50		11:00– 11:50	11:00– 11:50
20-200	Tennis Rm GYM		1:00– 1:50		1:00– 1:50	1:00– 1:50

The sample shows a class schedule for a student at Eastern College. The schedule lists each of the courses the student has chosen by name and number. It also shows at what times, on which days, and in which rooms the classes meet. You can see that this student starts school at 9:00 a.m. on Mondays, Wednesdays, and Thursdays, and at 10:00 a.m. on Tuesdays and Fridays. You can see that the student has a class at 10:00 a.m. every day — Art in Society on Tuesdays, Thursdays, and Fridays in room 3-3001, and German II on Mondays and Wednesdays in the Language Lab. Study the schedule and find as much information as you can from it. Practice reading movie schedules in a newspaper, train schedules, or television schedules.

E. **Telephone Book**

Telephone books are very useful reference sources. They list names, addresses, and phone numbers of people, businesses, and services. They are published once a year by the telephone company, and are distributed free of charge to anyone with a telephone. Telephone books provide information about making phone calls — local, long distance, operator assisted, or emergency. They tell you what to do for service and repairs. Usually, they contain local maps with the zip codes and phone exchanges listed.

1. **White Pages**

The telephone book with white pages is an alphabetical listing of people and businesses in a city or metropolitan area, their addresses, and their phone numbers. People without a phone or with a private number are not listed.

Example:

```
Mazulas Louis 123 Crescent Dr  . . . . . . 589-0364
Mc (See Also Mac)
McAdams Jane 8409 N Fremont St. . . . 695-0124
McAndrews Chas 239 S Pine Rd. . . . . . 631-0548
McCabe John 3401 W Kilbourn . . . . . . 739-0562
McCann Judy 5906 W Wilson. . . . . . . . 839-6150
McCarthy Lisa 7986 N. Harvard . . . . . . 549-8633
McCarty Pat 5391 S Lake Av. . . . . . . . 395-4067
```

As you can see from the white pages sample, the names are listed alphabetically, last name first. Following the name is the address and phone number. Some names have more than one common spelling: the phone book will bring this to your attention by listing the alternate spellings. Practice using a white pages directory by looking up the names of people you know. Your alphabetizing skills will be helpful now.

2. **Yellow Pages**

The telephone book with yellow pages lists businesses and services alphabetically by category, such as "Restaurants," "Hospitals," etc. If you want to find an entry, you must know what category the business would be listed under. Some businesses will be listed under more than one category, so be sure to check any possibilities. Within each category, the names of the businesses are also alphabetically listed.

Example:

▶ **Pianos—Supplies & Parts**

Smith Piano Service
      839 Ocean Dr 839-4160

▶ **Pianos—Tuning & Repairing**

Peyson Piano Shop
      9105 W Foster 765-0983

▶ **Pick-Up Coaches & Campers**

  (See Campers & Pick-Up Coaches;
  also Camping Equipment)

▶ **Picture Frames—Dealers**

Addison Framers
      56 E Huron 481-9657
Johnson's Picture Frames
      8901 S Shore 935-0935

As you can see from the yellow pages sample, the listings are alphabetical by category, then alphabetical by name of business within each category. You can also see that a reference is provided for a product that falls into more than one category. Again, your alphabetizing skills will be helpful here. Practice using the yellow pages by looking up several types of businesses, including some that fall into more than one category.

Choose the word or phrase that means the same or nearly the same as the <u>underlined</u> word.

1. to <u>compose</u> a letter

   a) destroy
   b) mail
   c) create
   d) type

2. a <u>modern</u> building

   a) rough
   b) ancient
   c) large
   d) new

3. a <u>lonely</u> corner

   a) solitary
   b) busy
   c) frightening
   d) wonderful

4. an interesting <u>debate</u>

   a) topic
   b) discussion
   c) encyclopedia
   d) word

5. a <u>delighted</u> feeling

   a) cranky
   b) sad
   c) happy
   d) excited

6. to have great <u>respect</u>

   a) size
   b) dislike
   c) honor
   d) forgiveness

Go on to the next page.

7. the young man's <u>vigor</u>
   a) fun
   b) strength
   c) slowness
   d) love

8. <u>excess</u> traffic
   a) swift
   b) crowded
   c) slow
   d) surplus

9. <u>compelled</u> to act
   a) trying
   b) afraid
   c) forced
   d) rushed

10. <u>submitted</u> to the other team
    a) passed
    b) substituted
    c) surrendered
    d) traveled

11. a <u>stationary</u> tractor
    a) quick
    b) not moving
    c) gigantic
    d) broken

12. to <u>encourage</u> the plant to grow
    a) force
    b) help
    c) hinder
    d) water

Go on to the next page.

13. <u>concern</u> over his health

    a) interest
    b) exercise
    c) nervous
    d) disgust

14. <u>positive</u> that is correct

    a) hopeful
    b) worried
    c) unsure
    d) sure

15. <u>inquire</u> at the next window

    a) ask
    b) exclaim
    c) purchase
    d) steal

16. an <u>argument</u> about the problem

    a) story
    b) peace
    c) dispute
    d) talk

17. <u>permission</u> to go to the party

    a) consent
    b) refusal
    c) directions
    d) escort

18. <u>avoid</u> the bridge

    a) stop at
    b) cross
    c) keep away from
    d) dislike

Go on to the next page.

19. <u>disgrace</u> his father
    a) reward
    b) dishonor
    c) love
    d) murder

20. your <u>opinion</u> about politics
    a) belief
    b) vote
    c) facts
    d) meaning

21. deep <u>affection</u> for her dog
    a) love
    b) disregard
    c) training
    d) worship

22. <u>recommend</u> the restaurant
    a) dislike
    b) frequent
    c) disapprove
    d) suggest

23. <u>omitted</u> his signature
    a) misspelled
    b) wrote
    c) remembered
    d) left out

24. <u>satisfied</u> the child's wishes
    a) pointed to
    b) disappointed
    c) hurt
    d) fulfilled

Go on to the next page.

25. a great <u>quantity</u> of flowers

    a) dozen
    b) amount
    c) length
    d) width

26. <u>additional</u> chairs

    a) hard
    b) extra
    c) many
    d) few

27. to <u>exhaust</u> yourself

    a) sleep
    b) tire
    c) ruin
    d) exercise

28. to have endless <u>patience</u>

    a) sharpness
    b) hope
    c) care
    d) endurance

29. in the <u>vicinity</u> of

    a) room
    b) distance
    c) corner
    d) area

30. a big <u>appetite</u>

    a) need
    b) meal
    c) desire
    d) fortune

Go on to the next page.

109

**For questions 31 to 50, mark your answer sheet for the
letter of the sentence that contains a spelling error.**

31. a) Marcus is a very intelligent parrot.
    b) What effect did the experiment have on the animals?
    c) My brother was so sick, we had to call a special physian.
    d) That was the most mysterious detective story I have ever read.

32. a) The teacher taught the class several important lessons.
    b) You shouldn't listen to harmful advice.
    c) The information in the chart is not acurate.
    d) Earth is the only planet that has life.

33. a) My favorite animals in the zoo are the monkeys.
    b) It is dangrous to walk down that alley after dark.
    c) Coffee makes me nervous and irritable.
    d) How much does gasoline cost in your town?

34. a) The mayor declared the city a disaster area.
    b) His cousin will be fiveteen on his next birthday.
    c) English was Beth's favorite subject when she was in high school.
    d) The escaped bear was captured and returned to the zoo.

35. a) My choice for the job was a friend from my neighborhood.
    b) We always have turkey for Thanksgiving dinner.
    c) There were over fourty cats living in that house.
    d) It was over ninety degrees on the night of the party.

Go on to the next page.

36. a) Jean reads three newspapers each Sunday morning.
    b) We had many visitors during the holiday season.
    c) The material looked like silk but was really man-made.
    d) The elderly woman who lives in the corner house is very lonly.

37. a) The television studio was temporarily closed.
    b) The wildlife refuge is open to the public.
    c) Peter's pumkin had the most unusual face.
    d) Take a more peaceful route to drive to the ocean.

38. a) The report will be greatly improved if you rewrite it.
    b) His automobile slipped on the slick pavement.
    c) That was the most exciteing movie I have ever seen.
    d) Hundreds of cars were stuck in a huge traffic jam.

39. a) The fruit salad had oranges, apples, pears, peaches, and berrys.
    b) We had so many guests for the wedding that we were not sure we had
       room for them all.
    c) My brother collects gold and silver antique buttons.
    d) I read a magazine article about the dangers of smoking.

40. a) The letter to the editor must be typewritten.
    b) The school band marched in the holiday parade.
    c) I told her it was wrong to be so jelous of her sister.
    d) Can you assist me with the lighting and scenery?

Go on to the next page.

41. a) There was a disturbance in the theater last night.
    b) Marie studied many foriegn languages in school.
    c) We studied many novels, plays, and poems in school.
    d) I have to memorize two famous quotations by Monday.

42. a) Paul had a cheese sandwich, a banana, and milk for lunch.
    b) Maureen measured the height and length of the dresser.
    c) The children brought their skates and sleighs on the winter vacation.
    d) The kind man lent me his hankercheif.

43. a) Officials put up a new statue in the center of the business district.
    b) The woman remembered to connect the wires in her car.
    c) The store sells handmade crafts, puzzles, and dolls.
    d) Laura feels there is too much waste in the federal goverment.

44. a) The train was scheduled to leave from track eleven.
    b) The doctor told Steve to stay in bed and drink lots of fluids.
    c) The number of birds that nest in those oak trees increases yearly.
    d) I sent away for a mail order catolog.

45. a) The brilliant vase was made of pure gold.
    b) Remember to visit the little girl in the hospital.
    c) The happiest person I ever met was my aunt's cousin.
    d) The drug stores deliver all medicin free of charge.

Go on to the next page.

46. a) What time did that serious accident occurr?
    b) Tom was the winner in the dance competition.
    c) My father was elected to the new school board.
    d) After the play, the audience clapped with enthusiasm.

47. a) The swimming pool closes in late August.
    b) It is unnecessery to drive all the way to Seattle.
    c) Lisa is opposed to the destruction of the famous building.
    d) The owners of the lodge welcomed the entire ski club.

48. a) The fireman suggested that everyone check his electrical wires.
    b) Cindy would not rest until she satisfied her curiousity.
    c) Jenny built a seven-foot snowman in front of the hospital.
    d) Ken exchanged his sweater at a nearby department store.

49. a) Ron has always preferred to work in complete silence.
    b) George sent his aunt a sympathy card when his uncle died last spring.
    c) Can the hotel accomodate another guest?
    d) The dance was held Friday night in the gymnasium.

50. a) The lawyer gave his annual report to the board this morning.
    b) The advertisement said that each coupon was good for one free quart of milk.
    c) Claire smelled a pecular odor coming from the kitchen.
    d) Find the volume of that cylinder.

Go on to the next page.

For questions 51 to 90, look for errors in capitalization, punctuation, or usage. If there is no mistake, mark "d" on your answer sheet.

51. a) You and me can go skating when the pond freezes.
    b) Charlotte sold seventeen boxes of cookies to Mrs. Waller.
    c) Stacy asked, "What is your favorite color?"
    d) No mistakes.

52. a) Susan rarely goes to the movies.
    b) Amanda a friend from North Carolina brought me a beautiful present.
    c) The farmer grows cherries, apples, peaches, and pears in the orchard.
    d) No mistakes.

53. a) The rain completely soaked he and me.
    b) The family sold their old furniture to him and me.
    c) My drama class begins at 2:45 p.m.
    d) No mistakes.

54. a) Jon shared the money among his seven workers.
    b) What time is your nephew's surprise party?
    c) After the fog cleared, a beautiful rainbow appeared in the sky.
    d) No mistakes.

Go on to the next page.

55. a) Keith felt wonderful after he won the race.
     b) We will be going to the circus on Saturday, the twenty first.
     c) Michael mailed gifts to three orphans in Asia.
     d) No mistakes.

56. a) After you have cleared the land, we planted the vegetables.
     b) Mitchell exclaimed, "Look out for the bus!"
     c) The man from the shop gave them and us a gift certificate.
     d) No mistakes.

57. a) Most plants need sunlight and water.
     b) Heather and Megan have a beautiful doll collection.
     c) Tim invited a friend to his summer house in Michigan.
     d) No mistakes.

58. a) Long distance telephone rates are cheaper after 5:00 p.m.
     b) Where did you stay when you visited Florida?
     c) Pass me the catsup, please.
     d) No mistakes.

Go on to the next page.

59. a) He won first prize in the swimming contest.
    b) Each of them speaks a second language.
    c) They hadn't visited Europe until last summer.
    d) No mistakes.

60. a) Did you not hear me?
    b) History is the most interesting subject I have studied.
    c) The elections will be held in November.
    d) No mistakes.

61. a) Nick bought gum, chocolate, licorice, and taffy at the candy store.
    b) "Watch out for the lion!" Cathleen yelled.
    c) After Katie swept the entire apartment, her brother will track in mud.
    d) No mistakes.

62. a) Karen and I left the restaurant at the same time.
    b) Beth is the happier of the two twins.
    c) Perry hid the book so good no one could find it.
    d) No mistakes.

Go on to the next page.

63. a) Mr. Randall gave Lilly and he the keys to the new car.
     b) Matt smiled happily after he learned the plane had landed.
     c) The argument is between you and me.
     d) No mistakes.

64. a) "Won't you ever learn?" he shouted angrily.
     b) The Eliott family moved from the north side of town to a house on
        Madison blvd.
     c) I don't agree with Daisy's views on economics.
     d) No mistakes.

65. a) The school fair will be held June 17th in the football stadium.
     b) Paula has a dream to be the first woman to travel to mars by rocket.
     c) After climbing all the way to the top of the mountain, Liz sat down
        to rest.
     d) No mistakes.

66. a) In order to catch the plane, haven't they better leave now?
     b) Yesterday, Mabel and Dot swam fifty laps.
     c) The package was placed under the mailbox that said Tom S. Fields.
     d) No mistakes.

Go on to the next page.

67. a) She looked very well after the operation.
    b) Invitations were sent to Robin, Alex, Simon, Jordon, and Bette.
    c) Pat exclaimed to his sister, "Watch out for that enormous dog!"
    d) No mistakes.

68. a) That book taught Leon an important lesson.
    b) The operator answered the telephone and said, "your call will be thirty cents."
    c) The science project doesn't have to be perfect in order to win a prize.
    d) No mistakes.

69. a) The dentist's name, Myra P. Hill, was printed in block letters on her new business cards.
    b) The baby monkey, the cutest animal in the zoo, is on display today.
    c) Of all the animals in the pound, the persian cat was the most beautiful.
    d) No mistakes.

70. a) Hey, watch out for the falling rock.
    b) Maria asked what time you will be home.
    c) Bridget passed me the cream and sugar.
    d) No mistakes.

Go on to the next page.

71. a) William could of been the best student in his class.
     b) Some people in my town haven't much money.
     c) I admired the blanket that Leah had knitted so beautifully.
     d) No mistakes.

72. a) Candace dropped him and me off in front of our house.
     b) Isn't it time for the baby's nap?
     c) The Andersons are very proud of they're seven children and
        fourteen grandchildren.
     d) No mistakes.

73. a) I had to wait five weeks to get an appointment with dr. Edwards.
     b) After the terrible blizzard, she and I helped the neighbors shovel
        their walks.
     c) This secret must be kept between the two of us.
     d) No mistakes.

74. a) There is the famous art museum.
     b) That painting in the gold frame is the more valuable of the two.
     c) Ain't that old car worth more than one hundred dollars?
     d) No mistakes.

Go on to the next page.

75. a) The boy hisself opened the two doors for the old ladies.
    b) Barb gave this cup to the winner of the marathon.
    c) After you have eaten dinner, come into the living room.
    d) No mistakes.

76. a) The twins performed well at their piano recital.
    b) You and they should meet me at the west intersection of Maple Avenue and Cedar Lane.
    c) My favorite Christmas story, "a Christmas carol," was written by Charles Dickens.
    d) No mistakes.

77. a) Regardless of how busy you are, you must still sleep and eat.
    b) The pharmacy closes at seven the rest of the shopping center closes at eight.
    c) This article is about the greenhouse effect.
    d) No mistakes.

78. a) Choose one of these or two of those.
    b) We are going to a movie first and shopping second.
    c) I spotted a robin bluejay woodpecker and finch in the forest.
    d) No mistakes.

Go on to the next page.

79. a) The squirrel shared the acorns between the four baby squirrels.
    b) The children had fun tobogganing yesterday.
    c) This is the best cheesecake I've ever eaten.
    d) No mistakes.

80. a) The newspaper had several articles about the candidate's speech.
    b) Their grandfather is ninety-two years old.
    c) His cold is worser than mine.
    d) No mistakes.

81. a) She began walking at the age of eight months.
    b) Can't we ever be good friends?
    c) Leo Tolstoy wrote the novel War and Peace.
    d) No mistakes.

82. a) There are four turtles in the lake.
    b) All in the boat knows how to swim.
    c) I will call you after I return from Boston.
    d) No mistakes.

Go on to the next page.

83. a) Why aren't you ever ready on time?
    b) My car, the small green one, has two flat tires.
    c) Bob asked the director, "what cue am I supposed to remember?"
    d) No mistakes.

84. a) Set the chair down in that corner.
    b) Those books were not on the shelf.
    c) He pays $23.95 for those slacks when they were on sale.
    d) No mistakes.

85. a) James r. Smead was a secret agent for ten years.
    b) I have read this book two times.
    c) We usually buy groceries on Thursday evenings.
    d) No mistakes.

86. a) The fire, an uncontrollable one, destroyed the whole town.
    b) Sharon is the prettiest sister in the O'Keefe family.
    c) Nell said "I voted for the Senator in the last election."
    d) No mistakes.

Go on to the next page.

87. a) This poster received a honorable mention for design.
    b) One of the girls surprised me with a gift.
    c) They go camping several times each year.
    d) No mistakes.

88. a) To avoid a traffic delay, we must leave early.
    b) My cousin, who lives in Germany, is coming to America next spring.
    c) The new shopping mall is called water tower place.
    d) No mistakes.

89. a) The tennis shoes don't be on display.
    b) He and she helped us move.
    c) We drove to Hannibal in six hours.
    d) No mistakes.

90. a) The boy had a scientific mind, so he wrote an essay called "the
       importance of oxygen" for English class.
    b) The recipe requires oatmeal, eggs, water, and nuts.
    c) I will be home earlier than usual today.
    d) No mistakes.

Go on to the next page.

Read this passage, and then answer questions 91 to 98.

A metal called beryllium is only one-third as heavy as aluminum. Because of its lightness and lack of density, beryllium should be an excellent material for making airplanes. However, no one has yet been able to make an airplane from beryllium. This is because when the metal is melted and poured into a mold through a process called casting, the finished product is very brittle. Also, when another element is added to the molten metal, the particles tend to cluster and gather into a ball. Therefore nothing can be evenly added to beryllium. The reason this happens is that gravity will not allow particles to settle evenly throughout this low-density metal.

Scientists concluded that if they could melt beryllium in a gravity-free environment, they might be more successful in casting the metal. They melted and cooled a sample of beryllium for four minutes during the flight of a rocket. The experiment was a success, and someday it may be possible to construct aircraft from beryllium.

Go on to the next page.

91. The best title for this passage is

    a) "An Unsuccessful Experiment."
    b) "Experiments in Rocketships."
    c) "Casting Metals."
    d) "Beryllium: A Possible Metal for Aircraft."

92. How long did scientists let the sample of beryllium melt and cool in the spaceship?

    a) seven hours
    b) four hours
    c) two days
    d) four minutes

93. Why did scientists choose to conduct their experiment in a rocketship?

    a) It is dark in a rocketship.
    b) There is no gravity in space.
    c) The beryllium is heavier in a rocketship.
    d) The metal melts better there.

94. What is it called when a metal is melted and pressed into a mold?

    a) clustering
    b) gravity-free environment
    c) low-density metal
    d) casting

95. One reason beryllium cannot be successfully cast is that

    a) it is a low-density metal.
    b) it is a heavy metal.
    c) it is too expensive.
    d) it is too hot.

96. What metal is a good material for making airplanes?

    a) heavy metals
    b) aluminum
    c) very dense metals
    d) molten metals

97. Beryllium is a poor metal for making aircraft because

    a) it is brittle.
    b) it is too light.
    c) it is shiny.
    d) it has no gravity.

98. What is a result of the experiment described in the second paragraph?

    a) All metals will be successfully casted.
    b) Gravity will disappear.
    c) Aircraft may someday be made of beryllium.
    d) All airplane parts will be made inside rocketships.

Go on to the next page.

Read this passage, and then answer questions 99 to 106.

"Look at all the snow!" exclaimed Jeff.

Jeff and his friend, Mark, were leaving a movie theater. They had just seen a three-hour movie. When they entered the theater, it had been snowing lightly. Now, three hours later, at least a foot of snow had fallen and it was still snowing hard.

"I hope we can get the car started," replied a worried Mark.

Jeff looked into the distance and saw a woman walking toward them.

"Can you help me?" she asked. "My car is stuck in a snow bank with two flat tires. I had to leave my dog alone in the car."

Mark looked nervously at his watch and said, "There is a service station a block south."

Jeff looked angrily at Mark and told the woman that they would help her. The three walked a mile down the road to the woman's car. A friendly collie barked with delight from the back seat. Two hours later the group had fixed the tires and freed the car from the snow bank. Everyone was cold and tired. The woman thanked the two boys and wrote down their names and addresses.

Three days later, Mark and Jeff both received a check for twenty dollars in the mail. Mark felt sheepish when he cashed the check. He vowed to be more generous in the future.

Go on to the next page.

99. Why did Mark tell the woman the location of a service station?

    a) He didn't need any money.
    b) He didn't know how to change a tire.
    c) Jeff was too cold to help the woman.
    d) He hoped she would ask for help there.

100. Why did Jeff get angry at Mark?

    a) Jeff wanted to see the movie again.
    b) Jeff didn't want the woman to ask anyone else for help because he wanted to receive a check from her.
    c) Jeff felt Mark was being selfish.
    d) Jeff loved fixing cars.

101. What is the main idea of this story?

    a) It is unsafe to drive during snow-storms.
    b) It is important to help people in trouble.
    c) People should pay others for their help.
    d) It is better to take care of only yourself.

102. Why did Mark feel sheepish when he cashed the check?

    a) His car wouldn't start.
    b) He knew the check would bounce.
    c) He felt he had to share the money with Jeff.
    d) He really hadn't wanted to help the woman.

103. How did the woman show her appreciation for the boys' help?

    a) She sent them a reward.
    b) She gave them a dog.
    c) She sent them a thank-you note.
    d) She wrote down their names and addresses.

104. What were Jeff and Mark doing during the snowstorm?

    a) going to the bank
    b) working at a service station
    c) walking a dog
    d) watching a movie

105. How long did it take everyone to fix the car?

    a) four hours
    b) three hours
    c) one hour
    d) two hours

106. What was wrong with the woman's car?

    a) It had flat tires and was stuck in a snowbank.
    b) Her dog was locked in the car.
    c) It wouldn't start.
    d) It was left at a service station.

Go on to the next page.

Read this passage, and then answer questions 107 to 114.

Robert Louis Stevenson was a novelist and poet born in Scotland in 1850. He wrote such famous stories as *Treasure Island* and *The Strange Case of Dr. Jekyll and Mr. Hyde*. As a little boy, Stevenson suffered from gastric fever and other illnesses. He spent much of his childhood in bed and spent little time in school. Later he wrote a famous book of poems, *A Child's Garden of Verses*. Many of the poems in this book told about the imaginary world he lived in and the games he played while a sick child. Stevenson's father was a lighthouse engineer and wanted his son to become one, too. However, Stevenson was not interested in engineering and studied law instead. This resulted in many arguments between Stevenson and his father.

When Stevenson was 23, he again fell ill and visited the coast of France to try to recover. While in France, he wrote travel books. In 1876, Stevenson fell in love with Mrs. Osborne, a divorced American woman. His family was horrified, but Stevenson, ill and poor, traveled to America to marry Mrs. Osborne. The couple had little money, and Stevenson tried living in a mining camp in California. Soon his family forgave him and sent the pair enough money to return to Scotland. Stevenson became sick many times again. Each time he traveled to a new place. He went to Switzerland, America, England, and the South Sea Islands. He never regained his health, but his travels gave him many ideas for stories and novels.

Go on to the next page.

107. What is the best title for this passage?

    a) "Stevenson's Family Argument"
    b) "The Happy Life of a Famous Writer"
    c) "The Life of Robert Louis Stevenson"
    d) "Stevenson's Marriage"

108. Stevenson spent much of his childhood

    a) in school.
    b) in bed.
    c) writing books.
    d) traveling in France.

109. Where was Stevenson born?

    a) Scotland
    b) England
    c) South Sea Islands
    d) America

110. How would you describe Stevenson's relationship with his father?

    a) stormy
    b) peaceful
    c) very cold
    d) full of hatred

111. Which is a famous book of poems written by Stevenson?

    a) *The Strange Case of Dr. Jekyll and Mr. Hyde*
    b) *Treasure Island*
    c) *A Child's Garden of Verses*
    d) *Kidnapped*

112. In which country did Stevenson write travel books?

    a) France
    b) Scotland
    c) Switzerland
    d) England

113. Stevenson went to America

    a) to marry Mrs. Osborne.
    b) to work in a mining camp.
    c) to see California.
    d) because he had much money to spend traveling.

114. Which statement is true about the life of Stevenson?

    a) He disliked travel.
    b) He was not a good writer.
    c) He spent much of his life traveling to new places to try to regain his health.
    d) He worked as a lighthouse engineer and a lawyer.

Go on to the next page.

Read this passage, and then answer questions 115 to 122.

Most people think an igloo is a snowhouse, but in Eskimo language, igloo means any kind of shelter. The most famous igloos are the snowhouses of the Canadian Eskimos. To construct an igloo, blocks of hand-packed snow are formed. These blocks are stacked into a spiral that becomes smaller and smaller as it goes up to form a dome. The structure has a tunnel entrance that is lower than the floor. Cold air is thus trapped in the tunnel. The house is heated by a blubber or seal-oil lamp. A small hole in the top of the igloo is used for ventilation. The outside cold air preserves the igloo's shape.

Eskimos furnish their snowhouses sparsely by building "furniture" right into the snow blocks. A raised platform of snow is covered with furs, and is used for sleeping and eating. Shelves are carved into the walls to hold dishes and utensils. Windows are cut into the wall of the dome and can be covered with ice or seal intestines. A few igloos contain a table and stove. A snowhouse that the average Eskimo family lives in is about 10 feet wide. An igloo used for ceremonies is 20 feet wide.

Go on to the next page.

115. The best title for this passage is

    a) "The Eskimo Snowhouse."
    b) "Eskimo Life in Canada."
    c) "The Use of Seal-Oil Lamps."
    d) "Different Types of Eskimo Houses."

116. What shape is a snowhouse?

    a) a cube with a triangular roof
    b) tunnel
    c) dome
    d) a circular hole

117. Which of the following is an igloo?

    a) platform of snow
    b) tunnel entrance
    c) tent
    d) a blubber lamp

118. The most famous igloos are built from

    a) blocks of sealskin.
    b) blocks of snow.
    c) a spiral of ice.
    d) blubber.

119. Why is the doorway of a snowhouse built lower than the floor?

    a) to aid sleeping
    b) to circulate cold air in the house
    c) to keep the house warm
    d) to make more room in the house

120. Where does an Eskimo family sleep?

    a) in the entrance
    b) on a shelf carved into the igloo's walls
    c) on a raised snow platform
    d) outside the igloo

121. Why doesn't the heat from the lamp melt the igloo?

    a) Cold air is trapped in the doorway.
    b) There is a hole in the roof.
    c) The air outside is so cold.
    d) An igloo has windows.

122. Which statement is true about Eskimo snowhouses?

    a) They have no windows.
    b) All igloos have a table.
    c) They have little furniture.
    d) They are completely dark.

Go on to the next page.

Choose the list that shows the words in alphabetical order.

123.
a) leather
leash
learning
leave
leaving

b) learning
leash
leather
leave
leaving

c) learning
leash
leather
leaving
leave

d) leave
learning
leash
leather
leaving

124.
a) package
pact
paddy
paddle
page

b) pact
package
paddle
paddy
page

c) package
pact
paddle
paddy
page

d) package
pact
paddle
page
paddy

Go on to the next page.

Choose the listing from the telephone book that shows the words in alphabetical order.

125.
a) A & B Jewelers
Antique Jewelers
Biway Jewelers
Brad & Mark Co.
Charms & Diamonds

b) Antique Jewelers
A & B Jewelers
Brad & Mark Co.
Biway Jewelers
Charms & Diamonds

c) A & B Jewelers
Antique Jewelers
Biway Jewelers
Charms & Diamonds
Brad & Mark Co.

d) Antique Jewelers
A & B Jewelers
Biway Jewelers
Brad & Mark Co.
Charms & Diamonds

126.
a) All Wood Tables
American Furniture
Andy's Home Mart
Apple Furniture Co.
Angela's Wood Shop

b) All Wood Tables
Andy's Home Mart
American Furniture
Angela's Wood Shop
Apple Furniture Co.

c) All Wood Tables
American Furniture
Andy's Home Mart
Angela's Wood Shop
Apple Furniture Co.

d) American Furniture
All Wood Tables
Andy's Home Mart
Angela's Wood Shop
Apple Furniture Co.

Go on to the next page.

Use the directions below to answer questions 127 to 130.

HOW TO MAKE TOFFEE

1. Place 1 cup of butter in a 2-quart saucepan, and melt over medium heat.

2. Add 1 cup sugar, 2 tablespoons water, and ¼ teaspoon salt to melted butter. Stir until mixture begins to boil.

3. Place a candy thermometer in the mixture. Stirring occasionally, heat mixture to 310° F.

4. When mixture is heated, remove from heat, and add ¾ cup ground nuts.

5. Very quickly pour hot mixture into a square cake pan and spread evenly. Let cool.

6. When the candy has hardened, break into pieces and store in an airtight container.

---

127. How can you tell when the mixture has reached 310° F?

    a) by using a timer
    b) by feeling the pot
    c) by using a candy thermometer
    d) by tasting it

128. What must you do very quickly when making toffee?

    a) pour the liquid mixture into a pan
    b) stir the mixture
    c) break the candy into pieces
    d) melt the butter

129. Which ingredient is <u>not</u> used in making toffee?

    a) nuts
    b) sugar
    c) salt
    d) honey

130. Which of the following would be the best to use to store the finished candy?

    a) a paper bag
    b) a tin box with a tight top
    c) a piece of wax paper
    d) a glass bowl

Go on to the next page.

Use the table of contents below to answer questions 131 to 134.

TABLE OF CONTENTS

131. Which chapter tells about the treasure map?

   a) Chapter 2
   b) Chapter 4
   c) Chapter 1
   d) Chapter 5

132. The introduction begins on what page?

   a) 41
   b) 19
   c) ix
   d) 1

133. Which chapter begins on page 76?

   a) The First Search Party
   b) The Jewels
   c) The Second Search Party
   d) Necessary Equipment

134. Which chapter describes the equipment one must bring on the treasure hunt?

   a) Chapter 3
   b) Chapter 1
   c) Chapter 4
   d) Chapter 2

Go on to the next page.

135. Which reference source would tell you the beginning page of a chapter of a book?

  a) Glossary
  b) Index
  c) Table of Contents
  d) Introduction

136. Which reference source would tell you who has swum the farthest in the world?

  a) atlas
  b) card catalog
  c) dictionary
  d) *Guinness Book of World Records*

137. Which reference source would tell you where to find three magazine articles about Iran?

  a) *Readers' Guide to Periodical Literature*
  b) card catalog
  c) encyclopedia
  d) dictionary

138. Which reference source would contain a <u>short</u> description of the life of Susan B. Anthony?

  a) *Guinness Book of World Records*
  b) atlas
  c) index
  d) biographical dictionary

139. Which reference source would list three books about gardening?

  a) card catalog
  b) encyclopedia
  c) dictionary
  d) *Readers' Guide to Periodical Literature*

140. Which reference source would tell you four synonyms for the word "flower"?

  a) thesaurus
  b) dictionary
  c) encyclopedia
  d) glossary

141. Which reference source would tell you what body of water Italy borders?

  a) *Guinness Book of World Records*
  b) dictionary
  c) card catalog
  d) atlas

142. Which reference source would tell you what the population of Thailand is?

  a) thesaurus
  b) encyclopedia
  c) biographical dictionary
  d) atlas

Go on to the next page.

Use the dictionary page entries below to answer questions 143 to 146.

DICTIONARY PAGE

frib·ble (frib´əl), *adj.* of little value. *n.* **1.** a person who wastes time. **2.** an unimportant thought.

fric·as·see (frik´ə sē´), *n.* a stew of meat, served in a sauce.

fric·tion (frik´shən), *n.* **1.** a rubbing. **2.** disagreement.

frig´ate (frig´it), *n.* a sailing ship.

143. Which word can mean "disagreement"?

   a) frigate
   b) fricassee
   c) fribble
   d) friction

144. Which word has three syllables?

   a) fricassee
   b) frigate
   c) friction
   d) fribble

145. What part of speech is the word "fribble"?

   a) noun and adjective
   b) verb
   c) adjective only
   d) noun only

146. What is a "frigate"?

   a) a thought
   b) a disagreement
   c) a stew
   d) a ship

Go on to the next page.

Use the index below to answer questions 147 to 150.

```
┌─────────────────────────────────────────────┐
│                BOOK INDEX                    │
│                                              │
│  Education                                   │
│        colonies. . . . . . . . . . . . 54-59 │
│        19th century . . . . . . . . 511, 513 │
│  Eisenhower, Dwight D.                        │
│        cabinets. . . . . . . . . . 601, 609-611│
│        later years . . . . . . . . . . 607   │
│  Elections                                   │
│        1796 . . . . . . . . . . . . . 74-76  │
│        1840 . . . . . . . . . . . . 501-504  │
│        1916 . . . . . . . . . . . . 544-546  │
│  Emerson, Ralph. . . . . . . . . 496, 497, 500-502│
└─────────────────────────────────────────────┘
```

147. What pages would tell you about Eisenhower's cabinets?

    a) 511, 513
    b) 607
    c) 544-546
    d) 601, 609-611

148. To find out about education in the colonies, you would look on pages

    a) 501-504.
    b) 511, 513.
    c) 74-76.
    d) 54-59.

149. What topic would you find on pages 501-504?

    a) the later years of Eisenhower
    b) the election of 1840
    c) education in the 19th century
    d) the election of 1796

150. What pages would tell you about Emerson?

    a) 496, 497, 500-502
    b) 544-546
    c) 511, 513
    d) 609-611

Go on to the next page.

Use the map below to answer questions 151 to 154.

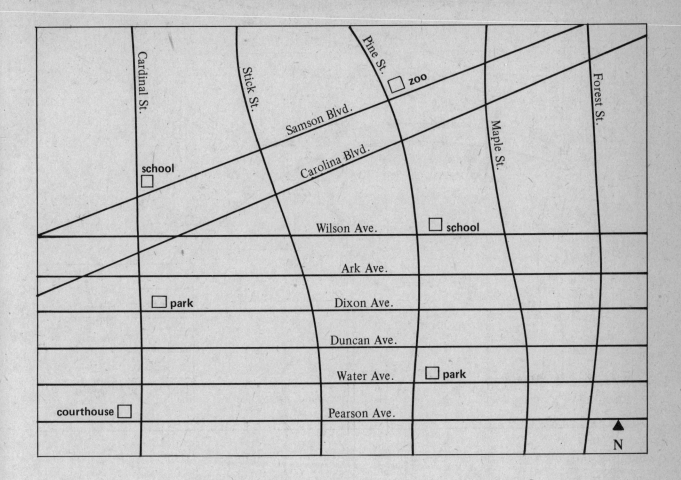

151. Which street is two streets south of Duncan Ave.?

    a) Pearson Ave.
    b) Water Ave.
    c) Ark Ave.
    d) Wilson Ave.

152. What is located at the intersection of Pine St. and Samson Blvd.?

    a) a school
    b) a zoo
    c) a park
    d) a courthouse

153. In which direction does Maple St. run?

    a) northeast
    b) east-west
    c) southwest
    d) north-south

154. Which of the following streets does Carolina Blvd. cross?

    a) Dixon Ave.
    b) Cardinal St.
    c) Water Ave.
    d) Pearson Ave.

Go on to the next page.

Use the map below to answer questions 155 to 158.

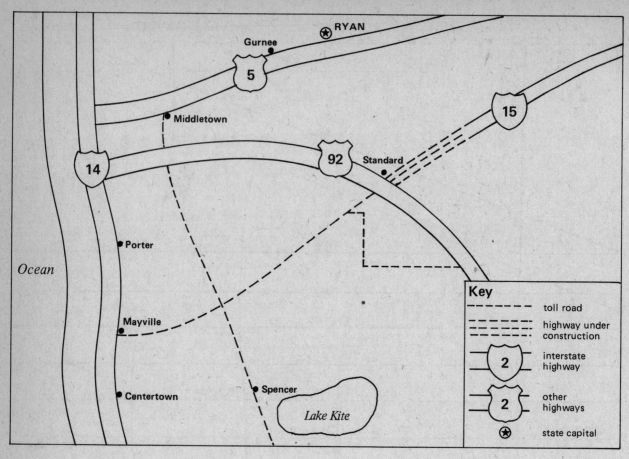

155. What highway would you travel to go from Gurnee to the state capital?

    a) Highway 92
    b) a tollway
    c) Interstate Highway 15
    d) Highway 5

156. Which highway would you travel to take a scenic drive along the ocean?

    a) Interstate Highway 14
    b) Interstate Highway 15
    c) Highway 5
    d) Highway 92

157. Which highway would be the most difficult on which to travel?

    a) Highway 92
    b) a tollway
    c) Highway 5
    d) Interstate 15

158. Which highway would you take to travel from Middleton to Lake Kite?

    a) Highway 5
    b) Interstate 14
    c) the tollway
    d) Interstate 15

Go on to the next page.

Use the advertisement below to answer questions 159 to 162.

GENTLE

ear drops
to relieve pain from earaches

DIRECTIONS: Use directly from bottle. Tilt head sideways and squeeze bottle so 2-4 drops enter the ear. Tip of bottle should not enter the ear. Keep head tilted so drops remain in ear for 3 minutes. Repeat with other ear. Repeat three times daily for at least one week.

CAUTION: Call physician if redness, pain, or swelling increases.

**AVOID CONTACT WITH EYES OR MOUTH.
STORE BOTTLE IN A COOL, DARK PLACE.**

---

159. What condition does this medicine help?

    a) cleaning the ears
    b) swelling of the eyes
    c) redness around the mouth
    d) earaches

160. How many drops should enter the ear?

    a) 1
    b) 3
    c) 2-4
    d) 2-3

161. How long should you use this medicine?

    a) 3 minutes
    b) 3 days
    c) one week
    d) 2-4 weeks

162. Which statement is <u>false</u> about this medicine?

    a) The drops should be placed in a container and then applied to the ear.
    b) The bottle should be stored in a cool, dark place.
    c) A doctor should be contacted if pain persists.
    d) The drops should be placed in both ears.

Go on to the next page.

Use the label below to answer questions 163 to 166.

```
┌─────────────────────────────────────┐
│                                     │
│         APPAREL LABEL               │
│                                     │
│  50% COTTON      RN406      SIZE 8  │
│  50% POLYESTER                      │
│                                     │
│  WASH  BY  HAND  OR  MACHINE.       │
│  WASH  WARM.  LINE  OR  TUMBLE      │
│  DRY.                               │
│                                     │
└─────────────────────────────────────┘
```

163. According to the label, what is this article
of clothing made of?

  a) entirely of polyester
  b) entirely of cotton
  c) part cotton, part polyester
  d) linen

164. What size is this article of clothing?

  a) size 10
  b) size 6
  c) size 40
  d) size 8

165. How should you wash this article of
clothing?

  a) machine wash at any temperature
  b) dry clean only
  c) wash by hand or machine in warm
     water
  d) wash in very cold water

166. Which is the correct way to dry this
garment?

  a) on a clothesline or in a dryer
  b) with an iron
  c) at the dry cleaners
  d) in a very hot dryer

Go on to the next page.

DEPARTMENT OF HEALTH AND HUMAN SERVICES
SOCIAL SECURITY ADMINISTRATION

Form Approved
OMB No. 0960-0066

FORM SS-5 — APPLICATION FOR A
SOCIAL SECURITY NUMBER CARD
(Original, Replacement or Correction)

MICROFILM REF. NO. (SSA USE ONLY)

Unless the requested information is provided, we may not be able to issue a Social Security Number (20 CFR 422.103(b))

INSTRUCTIONS
TO APPLICANT

Before completing this form, please read the instructions on the opposite page. You can type or print, using pen with dark blue or black ink. Do not use pencil.

		First	Middle	Last
NAA	NAME TO BE SHOWN ON CARD			
NAB	FULL NAME AT BIRTH (IF OTHER THAN ABOVE)	First	Middle	Last
ONA	OTHER NAME(S) USED			

1

2

STT	MAILING ADDRESS	(Street/Apt. No., P.O. Box, Rural Route No.)	
CTY STE ZIP	CITY	STATE	ZIP CODE

3 CSP CITIZENSHIP (Check one only)
- a. U.S. citizen
- b. Legal alien allowed to work
- c. Legal alien not allowed to work
- d. Other (See instructions on Page 2)

4 SEX / SEX
- Male
- Female

5 ETB RACE/ETHNIC DESCRIPTION (Check one only) (Voluntary)
- a. Asian, Asian-American or Pacific Islander (Includes persons of Chinese, Filipino, Japanese, Korean, Samoan, etc., ancestry or descent)
- b. Hispanic (Includes persons of Chicano, Cuban, Mexican or Mexican-American, Puerto Rican, South or Central American, or other Spanish ancestry or descent)
- c. Negro or Black (not Hispanic)
- d. North American Indian or Alaskan Native
- e. White (not Hispanic)

6 DOB DATE OF BIRTH — MONTH / DAY / YEAR

7 AGE PRESENT AGE

8 PLB PLACE OF BIRTH — CITY / STATE OR FOREIGN COUNTRY

9
MNA	MOTHER'S NAME AT HER BIRTH	First	Middle	Last (her maiden name)
FNA	FATHER'S NAME	First	Middle	Last

PNO a. Have you or someone on your behalf applied for a social security number before? ☐ No ☐ Don't Know ☐ Yes

Molly Rose Elkins was born on June 1, 1970, in Providence, Rhode Island. Her mother's name is Mary Ellen Ross Elkins. Her father's name is Robert Michael Elkins. She lives at 17 E. Delaware Place, Elizabeth, New York 10956.

167. What answer would Molly give for the first line of question 1?

a) Molly Rose
b) Molly Rose Elkins
c) Mary Ellen Ross
d) Molly Elkins

168. What answer would Molly give for question 2?

a) Elizabeth, New York 10956
b) Providence, Rhode Island
c) 17 E. Delaware Place, Elizabeth, New York 10956
d) 17 E. Delaware Place

169. What answer would Molly give for the second line of question 9?

a) Robert M. Elkins
b) Michael Elkins
c) Robert Michael Elkins
d) Robert Elkins

170. What answer should Molly give for the first line of question 9?

a) Mary Ross
b) Mary Ellen Ross Elkins
c) Mary Ross Elkins
d) Mary Ellen Ross

Go on to the next page.

143

Use the driver's license below to answer questions 171 to 174.

DRIVER'S LICENSE (Back Side)

RESTRICTION CODES	Restriction(s)	Class	Donor
1. CORRECTIVE EYE LENSES			Seal
2. LEFT OUTSIDE MIRROR	**1**	**B**	
3. DAYLIGHT DRIVING ONLY			Area
4. AUTOMATIC TRANSMISSION	**4**		
5. BUILT UP SEAT CUSHION OR POWER SEAT			Emergency Medical Information
6. OTHER — AS INDICATED			Seal
	Blood Type Rh Factor	**O neg.**	Area

DRIVERS LICENSE CLASSIFICATIONS

CLASS A - ANY MOTOR VEHICLE THROUGH 8,000 LBS GROSS WEIGHT EXCEPT CLASS L OR M

CLASS B - ANY MOTOR VEHICLE THROUGH 16,000 LBS GROSS WEIGHT EXCEPT CLASS L OR M

CLASS C - ANY MOTOR VEHICLE EXCEPT TRUCK TRACTOR-SEMITRAILER COMBINATIONS, STINGER STEERED SEMITRAILERS, OR CLASS L OR M

CLASS D - ANY MOTOR VEHICLE EXCEPT CLASS L OR M

CLASS L - ONLY MOTOR DRIVEN CYCLES (LESS THAN 150 CCs)

CLASS M - ONLY MOTORCYCLES AND MOTOR DRIVEN CYCLES

171. What is the classification of this driver's license?

    a) O neg.
    b) B
    c) 14
    d) C

172. Restriction number 4 means this driver

    a) is nearsighted.
    b) is handicapped.
    c) must have a car with automatic transmission.
    d) has the use of only one hand.

173. Which statement is not true about this driver?

    a) He can drive a van.
    b) He wears glasses.
    c) He can drive an automobile.
    d) He can drive a motorcycle.

174. Why might a driver have restriction number 3?

    a) is a poor driver
    b) wears contact lenses
    c) is under 15 years of age
    d) poor vision at night

Go on to the next page.

Use the ads below to answer questions 175 to 178.

ADVERTISEMENTS

Help Wanted

Dog Walker, walk large, well-trained German Shepherd every afternoon for 1 hour. Perfect job for high school student. Must like animals. Call Pat, 667-4000, evenings.

Gardener, take care of lawn, trees, hedges. Summers only. $7.50 an hour. References necessary. Write Mrs. E. Richey, P.O. Box 45, Elmond, Wis.

Ice Cream Vendor, sell refreshments at High School football games. No experience necessary. Must be available every Saturday Sept. - Dec. Apply in person Wednesday, 3:00, at Emerson High School.

Zoo Worker, volunteer position in children's zoo. Good experience for future zookeepers. Experience with animals a plus. Call the zoo office, 753-4337.

---

175. For which job would you receive no salary?

    a) gardener
    b) ice cream vendor
    c) zoo worker
    d) dog walker

176. For which job would you work at a school?

    a) dog walker
    b) zoo worker
    c) ice cream vendor
    d) gardener

177. Which job requires that you apply by letter?

    a) gardener
    b) dog walker
    c) zoo worker
    d) ice cream vendor

178. Which job requires that you only work during the fall?

    a) dog walker
    b) zoo worker
    c) ice cream vendor
    d) gardener

Go on to the next page.

Use the ad below to answer questions 179 to 182.

CLASSIFIED ADS

HOUSE FOR RENT: 4 bedrooms, fireplace, large kitchen, 2 baths, finished basement, near schools, transportation. $1000/mo. including heat and electricity. Option to buy. Call T. Hatter, 564-3120 or 564-3121, days.

---

179. How many bathrooms does this house have?

    a) 4
    b) 2
    c) 1
    d) 3

180. What is the monthly rent for this house?

    a) $1,000 plus heat and electricity
    b) $1,000
    c) $2,000
    d) $12,000

181. Which statement is <u>not</u> true about this house?

    a) It is located near a school.
    b) It has a fireplace.
    c) You cannot buy this house now.
    d) It has a large kitchen.

182. When should you call to find out about this house?

    a) during the morning
    b) during the evening
    c) late at night
    d) you should write T. Hatter

Go on to the next page.

Use the information below to answer questions 183 and 184.

```
┌─────────────────────────────────────────┐
│         SAVE 25¢ on each of              │
│                                          │
│   THESE CANDY BARS WITH COUPON           │
│                                          │
│      1)  crisp wafer bar                 │
│      2)  peanut butter bar               │
│      3)  caramel chocolate bar           │
│      4)  dark chocolate bar              │
│      5)  milk chocolate piece            │
│                                          │
│      ─────────────────────────────       │
│                                          │
│          TOTAL SAVINGS                   │
│             $1.25                        │
└─────────────────────────────────────────┘
```

183. If you presented a coupon with your
     purchase of a peanut butter bar, how
     much money would you save?

     a) $.30
     b) $.50
     c) $1.25
     d) $.25

184. If you bought all five chocolate bars
     with a coupon, how much money
     would you save?

     a) $.25
     b) $1.25
     c) $1.00
     d) $1.01

Go on to the next page.

Use this train schedule to answer questions 185 to 188.

Departs from	Train Number	Departure Time	Arrives at	Arrival Time
125th St.	11	7:05 a.m.	195th St.	7:30 a.m.
130th St.	12	9:30 a.m.	bus depot	10:30 a.m.
56th St.	9	11:00 a.m.	81st St.	11:15 a.m.
94th St.	7	3:00 p.m.	Harrison St.	4:15 p.m.
42nd St.	4	5:30 p.m.	87th St.	6:00 p.m.

185. What train arrives at Harrison St. at 4:15 p.m.?

    a) #4
    b) #9
    c) #7
    d) #11

186. How long does it take train number 12 to travel from 130th St. to the bus depot?

    a) one-half hour
    b) forty-five minutes
    c) fifteen minutes
    d) one hour

187. What time does the number 4 train depart?

    a) 6:00 p.m.
    b) 5:30 p.m.
    c) 5:30 a.m.
    d) 3:00 p.m.

188. Where does the train that arrives at 81st St. at 11:15 a.m. depart from?

    a) 56th St.
    b) 130th St.
    c) 94th St.
    d) Harrison St.

Go on to the next page.

Use the program listing below to answer questions 189 to 192.

```
Morning

5:30    2  Farmer's News
6:00    2  The Mouse in the House (cartoons)
        7  Super Family (R)
        9  Movie "Tiger Escapes" (see Movie
           Guide)
       11  News
6:30    2  Movie "The Nest" (see Movie Guide)
        7  Gardening News
        9  Talk in the Morning Topic: Knitting
       11  Exercises
```

189. What show seen at 6:00 is a repeat?

a) The Mouse in the House
b) News
c) Super Family
d) "Tiger Escapes"

190. Where would you look to learn more about the movie, "The Nest"?

a) in the newspaper
b) on channel 9
c) in the Movie Guide
d) on channel 11

191. What will be discussed on the talk show, "Talk in the Morning"?

a) gardens
b) exercises
c) knitting
d) cartoons

192. What time do the cartoons begin?

a) 7:00
b) 5:30
c) 6:30
d) 6:00

Go on to the next page.

Use the phone book entries below to answer questions 193 to 196.

```
                    WHITE PAGES


Starr G M 325 S Oak Ave . . . . . . . . . . 943-1100
   Child's Teleph 325 S Oak Ave . . . . . 943-1101
Stary Peggy 110 N Apple Blvd . . . . . . . 241-9987
State Wide Realty—
   Agents—
   Parkside 7439 Memorial Plaza . . . . . 366-1234
   Ridgewood 901 N 1st Ave . . . . . . . . 599-0431
Statton John J 125 W Peterson . . . . . . 104-2131
   Teen's Teleph 125 W Peterson . . . . . 104-9107
Stauffer Carl Z 19 E Huron . . . . . . . . 641-0117
```

193. What is the phone number of the Ridge-wood agent of State Wide Realty?

   a) 599-0431
   b) 366-1234
   c) 104-2131
   d) 241-9987

194. What is the telephone number of the Starr's child?

   a) 943-1100
   b) 943-1101
   c) 104-9107
   d) 104-2131

195. Whose telephone number is 241-9987?

   a) G. M. Starr
   b) Peggy Stary
   c) John Statton
   d) State Wide Realty

196. Who lives at 19 E. Huron?

   a) John Statton
   b) Carl Stauffer
   c) Peggy Stary
   d) G. M. Starr

Go on to the next page.

Use the phone book entries below to answer questions 197 to 200.

YELLOW PAGES

▶ **Florists—Retail**
AL'S FLOWERLAND
    14 W 97th St 222-0001
Beck's Shop of Flowers
    434 Agatha St. 794-7761

▶ **Flower Bulbs & Seeds**
    (See Seeds & Bulbs)

▶ **Flowers—Artificial**
    (See Artificial Flowers, Plants & Trees)

▶ **Foods—Carry Out**
Andy's Pizza
    74 North Ave 646-1987
BIG HAMBURGER SHOP
    919 N Laramie 917-2345
Chinese Take-Out
    43 E 85th St. 431-7401

197. What heading would you look up to buy some artificial flowers?

    a) Artificial
    b) Flowers
    c) Artificial Flowers, Plants & Trees
    d) Party Goods

198. What is the address of Al's Flowerland?

    a) 74 North Ave.
    b) 434 Agatha St.
    c) 14 W. 97th St.
    d) 43 E. 85th St.

199. What is the telephone number for Andy's Pizza?

    a) 431-7401
    b) 917-2345
    c) 794-7761
    d) 646-1987

200. What heading would you look up to find flower bulbs and seeds?

    a) Bulbs
    b) Flowers
    c) Plants & Trees
    d) Seeds & Bulbs

1. c	6. c	11. b	16. c	21. a	26. b
2. d	7. b	12. b	17. a	22. d	27. b
3. a	8. d	13. a	18. c	23. d	28. d
4. b	9. c	14. d	19. b	24. d	29. d
5. c	10. c	15. a	20. a	25. b	30. c

	incorrect	correct		incorrect	correct		incorrect	correct
31. c	physian	physician	38. c	exciteing	exciting	45. d	medicin	medicine
32. c	acurate	accurate	39. a	berrys	berries	46. a	occurr	occur
33. b	dangrous	dangerous	40. c	jelous	jealous	47. b	unnecessery	unnecessary
34. b	fiveteen	fifteen	41. b	foriegn	foreign	48. b	curiousity	curiosity
35. c	fourty	forty	42. d	hankercheif	handkerchief	49. c	accomodate	accommodate
36. d	lonly	lonely	43. d	goverment	government	50. c	pecular	peculiar
37. c	pumkin	pumpkin	44. d	catolog	catalog			

51. a incorrect: You and me can go skating when the pond freezes.
　　　　correct: You and I can go skating when the pond freezes.
52. b incorrect: Amanda a friend from North Carolina brought me a beautiful present.
　　　　correct: Amanda, a friend from North Carolina, brought me a beautiful present.
53. a incorrect: The rain completely soaked he and me.
　　　　correct: The rain completely soaked him and me.
54. d No mistakes.
55. b incorrect: We will be going to the circus on Saturday, the twenty first.
　　　　correct: We will be going to the circus on Saturday, the twenty-first.
56. a incorrect: After you have cleared the land, we planted the vegetables.
　　　　correct: After you have cleared the land, we will plant the vegetables.
　　　　or: After you had cleared the land, we planted the vegetables.
57. d No mistakes.
58. d No mistakes.
59. d No mistakes.
60. d No mistakes.
61. c incorrect: After Katie swept the entire apartment, her brother will track in mud.
　　　　correct: After Katie had swept the entire apartment, her brother tracked in mud.
　　　　or: After Katie sweeps the entire apartment, her brother will track in mud.
62. c incorrect: Perry hid the book so good no one could find it.
　　　　correct: Perry hid the book so well no one could find it.
63. a incorrect: Mr. Randall gave Lilly and he the keys to the new car.
　　　　correct: Mr. Randall gave Lilly and him the keys to the new car.
64. b incorrect: The Eliott family moved from the north side of town to a house on Madison blvd.
　　　　correct: The Eliott family moved from the north side of town to a house on Madison Blvd.
65. b incorrect: Paula has a dream to be the first woman to travel to Mars by rocket.
　　　　correct: Paula dreams of being the first woman to travel to Mars by rocket.
　　　　or: Paula's dream is to be the first woman to travel to Mars by rocket.

66. a incorrect: In order to catch the plane, haven't they better leave now?
       correct: In order to catch the plane, hadn't they better leave now?
67. d No mistakes.
68. b incorrect: The operator answered the telephone and said, "your call will be thirty cents."
       correct: The operator answered the telephone and said, "Your call will be thirty cents."
69. c incorrect: Of all the animals in the pound, the persian cat was the most beautiful.
       correct: Of all the animals in the pound, the Persian cat was the most beautiful.
70. a incorrect: Hey, watch out for the falling rock.
       correct: Hey, watch out for the falling rock!
71. a incorrect: William could of been the best student in his class.
       correct: William could have been the best student in his class.
72. c incorrect: The Andersons are very proud of they're seven children and fourteen grandchildren.
       correct: The Andersons are very proud of their seven children and fourteen grandchildren.
73. a incorrect: I had to wait five weeks to get an appointment with dr. Edwards.
       correct: I had to wait five weeks to get an appointment with Dr. Edwards.
74. c incorrect: Ain't that old car worth more than one hundred dollars?
       correct: Isn't that old car worth more than one hundred dollars?
75. a incorrect: The boy hisself opened the two doors for the old ladies.
       correct: The boy himself opened the two doors for the old ladies.
76. c incorrect: My favorite Christmas story, "a Christmas carol," was written by Charles Dickens.
       correct: My favorite Christmas story, "A Christmas Carol," was written by Charles Dickens.
77. b incorrect: The pharmacy closes at seven the rest of the shopping center closes at eight.
       correct: The pharmacy closes at seven; the rest of the shopping center closes at eight.
78. c incorrect: I spotted a robin bluejay woodpecker and finch in the forest.
       correct: I spotted a robin, a bluejay, a woodpecker, and a finch in the forest.
79. a incorrect: The squirrels shared the acorns between the four baby squirrels.
       correct: The squirrels shared the acorns among the four baby squirrels.
80. c incorrect: His cold is worser than mine.
       correct: His cold is worse than mine.
81. c incorrect: Leo Tolstoy wrote the novel War and Peace.
       correct: Leo Tolstoy wrote the novel <u>War and Peace</u>.
82. b incorrect: All in the boat knows how to swim.
       correct: Everyone in the boat knows how to swim.
83. c incorrect: Bob asked the director, "what cue am I supposed to remember?"
       correct: Bob asked the director, "What cue am I supposed to remember?"
84. c incorrect: He pays $23.95 for those slacks when they were on sale.
       correct: He pays $23.95 for those slacks when they are on sale.
           or: He paid $23.95 for those slacks when they were on sale.
85. a incorrect: James r. Smead was a secret agent for ten years.
       correct: James R. Smead was a secret agent for ten years.
86. c incorrect: Nell said "I voted for the Senator in the last election."
       correct: Nell said, "I voted for the Senator in the last election."
87. a incorrect: This poster received a honorable mention for design.
       correct: This poster received an honorable mention for design.
88. c incorrect: The new shopping mall is called water tower place.
       correct: The new shopping mall is called Water Tower Place.
89. a incorrect: The tennis shoes don't be on display.
       correct: The tennis shoes aren't on display.
90. a incorrect: The boy had a scientific mind, so he wrote an essay called "the importance of oxygen" for English class.
       correct: The boy had a scientific mind, so he wrote an essay called "The Importance of Oxygen" for English class.

91. d	121. c	151. a	181. c
92. d	122. c	152. b	182. a
93. b	123. b	153. d	183. d
94. d	124. c	154. b	184. b
95. a	125. a	155. d	185. c
96. b	126. c	156. a	186. d
97. a	127. c	157. d	187. b
98. c	128. a	158. c	188. a
99. d	129. d	159. d	189. c
100. c	130. b	160. c	190. c
101. b	131. a	161. c	191. c
102. d	132. c	162. a	192. d
103. a	133. c	163. c	193. a
104. d	134. a	164. d	194. b
105. d	135. c	165. c	195. b
106. a	136. d	166. a	196. b
107. c	137. a	167. b	197. c
108. b	138. d	168. c	198. c
109. a	139. a	169. c	199. d
110. a	140. a	170. d	200. d
111. c	141. d	171. b	
112. a	142. b	172. c	
113. a	143. d	173. d	
114. c	144. a	174. d	
115. a	145. a	175. c	
116. c	146. d	176. c	
117. c	147. d	177. a	
118. b	148. d	178. c	
119. c	149. b	179. b	
120. c	150. a	180. b	

Form B

Objectives	Item Numbers
I. LANGUAGE SKILLS	
A. Vocabulary	1, 2, 3, 4, 5, 6, 7, 8, 9, 10, 11, 12, 13, 14, 15, 16, 17, 18, 19, 20, 21, 22, 23, 24, 25, 26, 27, 28, 29, 30
B. Spelling	31, 32, 33, 34, 35, 36, 37, 38, 39, 40, 41, 42, 43, 44, 45, 46, 47, 48, 49, 50
C. Writing Skills	
1. Capitalization	64, 65, 68, 69, 73, 76, 83, 85, 88, 90
2. Punctuation	52, 54, 55, 57, 58, 70, 77, 78, 81, 86
3. Grammar	51, 53, 56, 59, 60, 61, 62, 63, 66, 67, 71, 72, 74, 75, 79, 80, 82, 84, 87, 89
II. READING SKILLS	
A. Literal Comprehension	92, 94, 95, 98, 103, 104, 105, 106, 108, 109, 111, 112, 116, 118, 120, 122
B. Inferential Comprehension	91, 93, 96, 97, 99, 100, 101, 102, 107, 110, 113, 114, 115, 117, 119, 121
III. REFERENCE SKILLS	
A. Alphabetical Order	123, 124, 125, 126
B. Following Directions	127, 128, 129, 130
C. Table of Contents	131, 132, 133, 134
D. Reference Sources	135, 136, 137, 138, 139, 140, 141, 142
E. Dictionary Entry	143, 144, 145, 146

Objectives	Item Numbers
F. Book Index	147, 148, 149, 150
G. Maps	
1. Street Maps	151, 152, 153, 154
2. Highway Maps	155, 156, 157, 158
IV. LIFE SKILLS	
A. Labels	
1. Medicine Bottle Labels	159, 160, 161, 162
2. Clothing Labels	163, 164, 165, 166
B. Forms	
1. Social Security Application	167, 168, 169, 170
2. Driver's License	171, 172, 173, 174
C. Advertisements	
1. Help Wanted	175, 176, 177, 178
2. For Rent	179, 180, 181, 182
3. Product Ads	183, 184
D. Schedules	
1. Train Schedule	185, 186, 187, 188
2. TV Schedule	189, 190, 191, 192
E. Telephone Book	
1. White Pages	193, 194, 195, 196
2. Yellow Pages	197, 198, 199, 200